THE DISHONEST NATURE OF SOCIALISM

THE DISHONEST NATURE OF SOCIALISM

Boris Browne

This book is distributed subject to the condition that it shall not, by way of trade or otherwise, be lent, hired out, or otherwise circulated without the publisher's prior consent in any form of binding or cover other than that in which it is presented.

Published by : T.E.Browne
ISBN 13: 978-0-9552051-0-7
ISBN 10: 0-9552051-0-7

9 780955 205101 >

To
All free citizens who
feel they have an innate
obligation to take
responsibility for their
own live...

CONTENTS

1. The Prescriptives

Having reached erroneous conclusions, it was hardly surprising then, to discover that Richard Dawkins the writer of the book, "The Selfish Gene" voted for socialists. In his defence however, he accepted that he was writing as a scientist and not as a philosopher. That was quite a necessary disclaimer for there can only ever be an understanding of human nature, through introspection and observation of our fellow man and not down the lens of a microscope. Even if Dawkins had been a philosopher, the chances of his providing us with some nuggets of wisdom assisting us in our public affairs, is highly unlikely.

In Britain today it is as if most of the philosophers since Socrates might as well have been carpenters or wainwrights. Most of their musings and preoccupations were on matters remote and nebulous and their conclusions imprecise and imperfect.

Even Aristotle in his assessment of goodness was it seems content with his own circular argument. He contended that actions are called good and temperate when they are such as a good and temperate man would do. However, he would have done well to have preoccupied himself with the consideration as to why we make such assessments as good and bad in the first place.

When we make a judgement of another and call them good we are making an assessment with regard to our own self-interest. Whether they are pacifying our own psyche in some way or materially assisting us. When we regard someone as bad they are causing us some disquiet or being disadvantageous to us in some material way.

Particular actions by one person can be considered very good or very bad simultaneously. Picture a man fervently supplying ammunition for an army besieging a city. To the inhabitants within the city walls in fear for their lives, he will be considered bad; and they would gladly take his life had they the fire power to do so. However the troops being supplied who stand to gain from the spoils within the city walls will consider him good.

There is an essential theoretical difference between this good and bad and Shakespeare's view of those two judgements. When two courtiers are involved in exchanges with Hamlet, one lets him know that there is no real news apart from the; world's grown honest. But having immediately dismissed this possibility, he questions their presence with him in prison. And when the other questions his belief regarding the prison, he replies –

"Why then, 'tis none to you; for there is nothing either good or bad, but thinking makes it so: to me it is a prison."

Even though this is an often quoted response it says nothing about either word, and does not explain why we feel it necessary to make such a distinction in our language in the first place. Both concepts play a powerful pivotal role in our lives. If we go with Shakespeare's view for the moment. If my family is being wiped out by the plague I may consider it good in the morning, and bad in the afternoon. Or if I have just lost all my worldly goods in a stock market crash, I may consider it bad in the evening and good in the morning. His finite truth stands alone and indisputable but it affords us nothing in our attempt to understand human nature.

From the moment we are born we scream and cry. The sudden drop in body temperature is decidedly uncomfortable. We instinctively broadcast our need for the restoration of our earlier comfort. From that declaration of our first need, we spend the rest of our lives striving to fulfil our other needs and making every conceivable move in easing our path through life. Everything that aids and abets us in the pursuit of that goal we consider good. Everything that obstructs us in that goal we consider bad.

If Socrates taught us anything, he taught us not to make assumptions. But politicians and academics regularly make assumptions. Even those who ostensibly set out to rigorously investigate a specific area of life, deviate into assumption having baulked at the truth. Or perhaps never had the courage to acknowledge the truth which was before them. The title of Dawkins' book, which I have mentioned earlier, intonated an investigation into a topic which had to have a relevance for our life form. But this was only given passing reference. Homo sapiens were invited in on a whim, and asked to leave on a whim, and were left in no doubt that the end that the party was not held in their honour. If the pertinence of the subject was not going to have a relevance for homo sapiens, then one wonders about the benefits of such a work. After all neither ants, kamikaze bees nor caddis flies were going to read his work. His microbiologists eye was focused with diligent discovery and analysis but he became tightly trussed up in the abode of the specialist. He came to tell us more and more about less and less.

However, to his credit he dismantled the 'good of the

species' argument with consummate ease. Those who held such a view were obviously not moved by the facts, least of all the facts regarding the history of man on this planet.

He aspired to produce

"an amplified and developed version of Neo-Darwinianism that could make everything about life fall into place, in the heart as well as the brain."

This aspiration dissipated pretty quickly, when, later he was perfectly comfortable in saying that we are an exceptional life form. He points to 'culture' as a way of hammering home this truth. However later he is moved to say:

"Nothing is more lethal for certain kinds of meme[1] than a tendency to look for evidence."

Had he seriously looked for evidence this 'culture' meme would not have come into being. The meme for blind faith was alive and well and replicating in Dawkins' consciousness.

He aspired to argue that a predominant quality to be expected in a successful gene is ruthless selfishness. He appropriately did not make a great distinction between the gene machine and the individual organism. Then the question has to be asked, are we not successful? Are we not; to use the words from the popular song; The Champions of the World? I feel every reasonable person would conclude that we are successful, and therefore perforce according to his reasoning ruthlessly selfish.

1 - a replicating unit of cultural transmission

therefore perforce according to his reasoning ruthlessly selfish.

In trying to eschew this fact Dawkins made some rather contradictory statements. He contended that:

"there are special circumstances in which a gene can achieve its own selfish goals best by fostering a limited form of altruism"

... however, if any gene, or gene machine achieves its own selfish goal by any of its actions, it is most definitely not altruistic, limited or unlimited.

He also expressed a desire to build a society in which individuals co-operate generously and unselfishly towards a common good. However, if any individual in his imagination performed any action towards a common good, presumably that individual by definition, forms part of that commonality and therefore the action could not be considered unselfish.

He discussed the behaviour of the parasol ants of South America. These sow fungus of a particular species in compost beds to be used for the digestion of leaves. Later the ants harvest and eat the fungi and feed them to their brood. He considered this arrangement to be mutually altruistic. However, it is clear that the ants were the masters; and the fungi their digestion machinery, which were not at liberty to get up and leave of their own volition. Considering what Dawkins set out to do; the word 'altruism' cannot be used as a trinket of decoration, when it has to be either an essential pillar in the argument or omitted entirely.

Further; he envisaged a situation where an animal finds a

clump of eight mushrooms. He followed through the mental processes and calculations the animal would go through with regard to the remaining five; having been able to consume only three of them. He concluded that since there may be a brother and cousin and some unrelated animals within earshot, it was best to give the food call. He concluded that this altruism on his part would pay his selfish genes.

I want to refer to the definition of altruism given by Dawkins:-

"An entity is said to be altruistic if it behaves in such a way as to increase another such entity's welfare at the expense of its own."

Clearly the animal who found the mushrooms was not involved in any such behaviour and his actions were not altruistic. How can anybody say that the action would pay his selfish genes and yet was altruistic? Such persons with such lack of insight, simply have to be socialists.

He went on the make the point that genes exert ultimate power over behaviour because of the way survival machines and their nervous systems are built. Nonetheless he also found it reasonable to say that we are not necessarily compelled to obey them. One wonders then how we; who are gene machines, can be motivated by some power which has to be somehow external to ourselves.

He then posed the question as to whether there was any experimental evidence for the genetic inheritance of altruistic behaviour. He concluded that there was none. Nevertheless he suggests that we should try to teach altruism. We as human beings who are composed of about one thousand million million cells, are supposed to assume that countless millions of those cells are there for a subversive purpose. In other words, after three thousand million years of evolution, with the beauty and perfection of nature all around us, we are supposed to believe that we are defective. The idea that we ought to teach altruism has to be one of the most absurd notions ever propounded; and not surprisingly, coming from the mind of a socialist sympathiser.

***

At this point I want to introduce the one and only character in this book. She is Vida. She is forty eight years of age. She is standing at a bus stop in the capital city. It is a late November evening; bitterly cold and raining. She has looked at her watch for the third time, it is 5.30.

2. On Altruism

It is firstly necessary to provide some appraisal of the word selfish. This conjures up the scene of a falling out between two eleven year old girls in a school playground, with accusation and counter-accusation of one being more selfish than the other. Interestingly, the older people become, the less and less they use this word. Perhaps as they live life they become aware of some truths that they would not publicly acknowledge. Perhaps this is what Churchill meant when he said:

"Men occasionally stumble over the truth, but most of them pick themselves up and hurry off as if nothing had happened."

But of one thing we can be absolutely certain – that no matter how vehemently one girl felt the validity of her accusation, there was not one tiny jot of difference between the degree of selfishness of either of them. For one to make an accusation of another, of being selfish, is the same as accusing the other of breathing. The accuser is often making the accusation because they feel they are being denied something they want. So the agitation arises in order to arouse in the other a feeling of guilt, in the hope that they would then accede to their demands.

This is not to say that one person does not act in an inconsiderate manner with respect to another. They certainly do.

However there is a world of difference between selfish and being inconsiderate. The word selfish carries with it the unspoken corollary of deprivation of another. It is a kind of moral see-saw with shame and virtue at either end. So the word selfish ought to be expunged from adult enlightened thinking and be replaced by the word self-interest. Should one of the girls in the playground spat, have eaten all her chocolates and not given any to her friend, then she may well have been regarded as inconsiderate by the other. But she behaved as she did because her psychological profile did not allow her to empathise with her friend's situation.

In her home when she was much younger her parents looked after themselves and gave little attention to their children. However, in the aggrieved girl's house, she was accustomed to affection, loving and sharing. Those two girls psychological profiles were incompatible and they would not be friends for long. Psychological profiles are highly distinctive and vary widely from one individual to the next. And it is when young children begin to recognise the incompatibility of their fellows that they shed those earlier friends, for those whose psychological profiles are most similar to their own.

Regardless of the inconsiderate behaviour of one of the girls, the aggrieved girl would have shared her chocolates if the situation were reversed. She would have done this because her psychological profile would have ensured that it was the natural thing to do. She could empathise with her friend as her parents empathised with her. To do otherwise would cause such an uncomfortable jarring of her psyche, that she would have been unable to behave as her friend did. The propensity of human beings to empathise with others is one of the most important aspects in our understanding of human nature.

One of the few things that distinguish ourselves from other primates is our more powerful brains and our ability to reflect on our condition. We have evolved as a life form with more powerful brains simply to enable us to overcome challenges from the environment, and other life forms, more effectively. Our brain affords us the ability to imagine. Were it not for the ability of our distant ancestors to fashion tools and weapons and indeed to fashion the necessary artifice to capture their prey, we would not be around to look back on their achievements. The thought, came before the artifice or artefact. Most of our thought is visualisation of what is imagined. So the aggrieved girl would have imagined herself in the other girl's position and would have shared her chocolates.

However what is of crucial importance to understand is that her motivation to behave in such a way is because it would be the easier of the two options. The girl who did not share was also motivated to behave as she did because it was the easier option for her. Both girls would always do what was in their own self-interest.

The price we pay for our larger and more powerful brains is the potential for psychological damage that can arise due to the mistreatment or neglect of the growing infant. The young brain is designed to learn and to learn fast from the new world. Hence if the child is loudly and aggressively berated, it feels; I deserve to be shouted at. If the child is ignored, it feels; I deserve to be ignored. If the child is physically abused it feels; I deserve to be physically abused. There is no reflective surface overlaying the consciousness of the new human being. Those invalidations are learned and internalised. The child cannot engage in a discussion

10

with another and ask;

"Do you think its right that I ought to endure this physical abuse because I am the only person available on whom my parents can vent their frustrations?"

No conversation can occur; and however unmerited the words, and unwarranted the abuse, the child accepts the former as true and the latter as right.

As Jean Piaget (1897-1980) demonstrated, the imagination, this vital aspect of our being, is slow to come to fruition. He came to the conclusion that; the imagination as the adult would understand it, does not reach completion until the child is around twelve years. His concern was with cognitive transitions or the manner in which the child comes to know about himself and the world in which he lives. It is not possible to access directly what a child of a few weeks or a few months thinks.

But Piaget found it was possible to infer something of the nature of the child's world from his behaviour. At around six months, he found, a child does not have any concept of the permanent existence of objects. When a toy falls from the child's hand it has disappeared from the universe. When it has formed an attachment with an object it desires, such as its feeding bottle, it demonstrates great desire when this is brought into view, but when it is removed from view the excitement and expectation disappear.

Since he has been born his mind has been active, he has been in the world of discovery, he has performed many actions on many objects, but yet at ten months he cannot distinguish his own actions from the objects, on which he has performed the action. If

11

he happens to be playing on the floor amongst his toys, and he lifts an upturned cardboard box and finds a ball, he may handle the ball for a while; but if someone takes the ball from his hands and puts it under a second upturned cardboard box further away while he is watching, he will lift the original cardboard box again to find the ball. His idea of object and place is complete if it coincides with his experience; but he has no concept that an object may be associated with different places.

One could imagine that when a good command of language is developed these little difficulties would be no more. But not so. Piaget found that by engaging in an experiment with one short wide tumbler and two tall narrow tumblers the child still had things to resolve. When he asks a five year old to slowly fill both tall glasses with beads, placing one at a time in each glass, he can get confirmation at the end that both glasses contain the same amount of beads. But when he pours the beads from one of the glasses, into the shorter glass, the child now believes that there are fewer beads in the shorter glass. Simply because it is lower. He can find out from questioning that the five year old is aware that no beads have been added or taken away, but he still holds to his belief that there are fewer in the lower glass. When a seven year old is asked to join in, he discovers that he has no difficulty realising that the shorter glass holds the same amount as the taller one. After questioning, he discovers that the seven year old came to this knowledge because he was able to imagine pouring the beads back into the taller glass. But were the electrical circuits in the brain of the seven year old allowing this imagination to take place, complete in other respects? Far from it.

In other experiments, which I update for present purposes, he took the seven year old into a room with three objects on a table in the middle. Those objects were a clock, a small television and a framed photograph. The child sits down at the table with the three objects placed at random but all facing him. Piaget then takes the child slowly around the table asking him to observe the objects as he moves. He sits him down again. Then a doll is placed in a highchair at the opposite end of the table and the child is asked what he considers the doll would be able to see from there. He is shown a series of pictures of the objects from different angles; but the only one he ever picks out, no matter where the doll is moved to, is the picture of what he himself sees. He cannot conceive that there is another viewpoint or reality than his own. It is between the age of eight and early teens that further electrical connections become activated enabling the young person to do what Piaget described as making that which is external, internal. Making tacit knowledge explicit knowledge. Or that which allowed the seven year old to juggle with the known facts and be able to say; "If I pour the beads back into the taller glass they will both be the same."

This apparently insignificant piece of mental juggling is the sign of the maturing imagination. And it is this imagination that has allowed homo sapiens to shape his environment unlike any other life form before him. Is it, one wonders, a coincidence that soon after the imagination is matured the human being begins to start the process enabling him to reproduce? When some human being first scratched symbols onto a soft clay tablet, they had to be in the imagination first. Would language ever have evolved if our remote antecedents had not been able to imagine that their fellow hunters would have been able to understand their utterances? If they could not imagine this, then why would they have uttered anything? A one month old dog or cat has the same five senses as a one month old baby. A new baby has no imagination. And it is the length of time it takes this to reach full maturity that demonstrates its newness in evolutionary terms. It is this that sets us apart, and not as some people believe, culture, or the remarkable personal likeness to an omnipotent deity.

Since the imagination is slow to complete formation the child cannot empathise. There is no safety valve. It cannot think; "If I was a parent; would I treat my child in this way? The child is not proactive in its interactions with its parents, it is the recipient of treatment from them. The child's sense of self is being moulded by its parents. When the child starts school a whole new vista of interactions opens up. Now amongst its own age group it is free to be an individual in its own right. It is now a doer, a giver, a taker, a talker, a listener, a reader, a writer, a screecher, a laugher, a player. The playground is a cacophony of noise where each child demonstrates their excitement in the awareness of their own individuality. When one boy is seen crying in the corner some children run over to comfort him, and try to find out why he is crying. But the children to run over will be the one's whose parents comforted them when they cried. As their imaginations are taking shape, their empathy begins.

***

The degree to which any individual has minor psychological problems or major psychological problems is determined by their experiences in their pre school years. Since everybody has a psychological profile as everybody has been affected in one way or another by their upbringing it is important to look at how this may arise.

I want to create an analogy between the psychological

profile and an electronic circuit. Even though electronics and psychology are not natural bed-fellows, it will suffice for clarification purpose. If we imagine a small electronic circuit about the size of a page with about two dozen interconnections. At the base of this circuit two strands lead up from a module called Life Force. At the top, two strands lead down from the module called – Needs, Ambitions, Fulfilment, Aggrandisement. All of the intervening circuitry between the lower and upper modules, is that which allows or enables the individual to pursue their ambitions, to obtain fulfilment, and aspire towards self improvement. The optimum size of all interconnecting strands is, we shall say, three millimetres in diameter. However, in some children parental behaviour will have constricted some to no greater than a human hair, causing others to inflate disproportionately. This serious imbalance will cause a myriad of personal difficulties in later life. But no person's circuitry will be in perfect balance, and there will be all manner of variations from the grossly imperfect to the near perfect.

However imperfectly the power is distributed from the life force; no individual ever consciously acts against their own self-interest. If they do not act against their own self-interest they must act in their own self-interest. Some commentators have tried to make the point that certain tribes exhibit selfishness while others exhibit altruism. This juxtaposition of two snap shots of two tribes from different continents makes no sense. If one exhibited apparent altruism it was because past experiences motivated them to behave in such a way as they had come to expect reciprocation, or other advantage. The other tribe did not give of their time, or their wares, or their hospitality as they did not see it was in their interest to do so.

It is this same lack of perspicacity that allowed a 'leading' British philosopher to front a broadcast on the altruism of starlings. He claimed that because they flock together the starlings at the extremities of the flock were altruistic in so far as they were prepared to sacrifice themselves to protect the birds in the centre.

It is almost painful to have to point out that in a flock of birds, it is impossible for some birds not to be at the extremities. Or does he imagine they took a vote or cast lots before leaving their previous resting place? Or perhaps he feels that only altruistic birds flock together to ensure survival of the greatest numbers following a swoop by some other birds of prey. But one has to say that birds that flock together provide a much better target than those that fly singly, such as blackbirds, thrushes or robins.

The pursuance of philosophy ought to be for the purposes of primarily gaining insight into human life and human behaviour. The philosopher's dalliance with the starlings was for the purposes of trying to prove something which he had already accepted as a truth regarding human beings. He wasn't able to interview the starlings or carry out any kind of meaningful experiment, but he was able to interview human beings. However, the results of this could lead to the disturbance of his own prejudice and the idea would not be followed through. It takes a certain amount of courage to confront the truth. And it is in the pursuit of this, that I humbly invite you, dear reader to participate. That is all of you who have not concurred with what I have said in relation to altruism so far. It would be very beneficial if all philosophy teachers, philosophy lecturers and senior lecturers in philosophy were to take part. The task is to take a pen and a blank sheet of paper, or several sheets, depending on your state of enlightenment and start to write down all the things you have done in your entire life which were not in your own self-interest. That is, all of your altruistic actions.

***

If you have written anything at all, those words are the materialisation of your own self-delusion. If you have written anything, you ask: "Why?" And having answered you ask why again. And having answered that you ask again: "Why?" And you will eventually have gone through a process of distillation to reach the purity of truth. It is only through the acceptance of truth that we can improve our world.

In the altruistic list some persons may well include charity or charitable works. But if the representative of a female religious order goes to work amongst the destitute in an Indian city, she is merely demonstrating that she believes completely what she has been told. Namely, that if she lives a life of denial of sensual pleasures and does 'good' works, she will go to heaven and enjoy everlasting happiness. Set against eternity, fifty or sixty years is a mere blink of an eye. Her pay-off will be considerable and her motivation to act is taken in her own self-interest.

What is quite remarkable is that the many millions who profess to believe in the same teaching do not act in a similar way. If you believe that railing against the use of contraception and thus ensuring more and more babies are born into a world of deprivation, disease and squalor, is doing 'good' works, then you will regard her as a 'good' person. Charitable giving is always carried out because of the mental activation of empathy. It is none

17

other than; If I were in his/her position, I would like someone to help me. Alongside this are the minor pay-offs of being considered by others a generous fellow, and the saying, which will face no challenge here: 'it is in giving that we receive.'

What has to be stressed even more strongly is that this does not mean that one person's actions cannot benefit others. They can and often do. But the primary motivation is the self-interest of the benefactor. If a wealthy man gives five million pounds to a museum, art gallery, or school, he does so because the next best alternative is to bequeath it to his nephew, who would probably lose it over two years in several casinos.

A case frequently used by those who think they have proved the contrary argument is that of the drowning individual. When one person comes upon a scene where another is drowning, the immediate thought is whether they are capable of saving the drowning person. If he feels he can, he jumps in and pulls the person ashore. The motivation for the action was the triggering of empathy. He thinks - if I was unable to swim and I was drowning, would I like someone to save me? Since the answer is in the affirmative, he takes the action. If those who make assumptions were to question him afterwards as to why he did it, they would hear something like, "I just had to, I couldn't ignore his cries for help; if I had walked on and left him to die, I couldn't live with myself." His pay-offs will be; the gratitude of his fellows and the rescued; the not insignificant sense of achievement and the absence of any guilt.

His empathy was immediately triggered because the imagination is never switched off. Everyone will regard the rescuer as a good person, simply because of their own ego transference to the position of the rescued. So all references to good and bad by me are in relation to me, and my self-interest. The imagination is never switched off because imagination is as much a facet of human consciousness as wool is of sheep.

So altruism does not exist. No human being has ever thought a thought or moved a muscle which was not in their own self-interest to do.

3. Honest Endeavour

It is true that along the spectrum of humanity there are wide variations between the psychopath and the philanthropist. But the seeds of those variations are sown in childhood. Ever since the ancient Greeks and beyond man has searched for truth. He has searched for explanations of all phenomena and pondered the meaning of our existence. We are drawn to this latter pursuit because of our ability to reflect on our condition. We can do this because we can imagine ourselves anywhere we like, at any time. If we left the supermarket two hours ago and are now home; we can visualise ourselves back there again. We can change all circumstances we encountered therein. We can change the check-out assistants for any persons we can visualise. We can imagine the building full of pineapples, elephants, or grand pianos. We can take ourselves out through the roof until we look back on a tiny building and keep on going until we can, thanks to images from space travel, look back on a blue and white globe getting ever smaller and disappearing as we move at speed into interstellar space.

I do not contend that this imagination sets us apart from other species in any spiritual sense, but is merely a by-product of our greater intelligence, which itself evolved, for improving our chances of survival. Hence if we do not start from authentic verifiable first principles we will have to continue to endure the vast tomes of philosophy which are generated because the writer set out on the basis of conjecture and supposition and with each word moved further and further away from the truth.

It has to be said that most philosophers set out with genuine and honest intentions in their pursuit of truth. Some were dishonest and I will say something of those later. Around two thousand five hundred years ago Anaximander who was driven by scientific curiosity reached some beliefs of extraordinary greatness given his tools of investigation. Having observed that his world and all the heavenly bodies were constantly in a state of change, he rightly concluded that the Earth as he perceived it did not exist at one time and would cease to exist at some time in the future. He reasoned that all matter was without boundary or limit and that this matter was the stuff from which all the distant worlds were made. He saw that as they originated from the infinite, they would return to the infinite. Most astrophysicists today hold to the big bang theory and therefore a return to singularity seems a highly plausible supposition. And once that is a circumstance that could not persist indefinitely a return to another big bang is highly likely. The possibility that this could be a scenario going on ad infinitum is more plausible than some other theories.

He also contended that the earliest living organisms came to life in moisture enclosed in thorny bark. He correctly concluded that human beings evolved from creatures of another sort. Since he did not have an enormous pool of evidence from predecessors or powerful telescopes to assist him; his greatness can be measured against the fact that hundreds of millions of people today do not believe his latter assertion, despite having all the evidence available to them.

Some seventy years later Heracleitus maintained that there was a fundamental equilibrium in the Universe; and that such a balance was maintained as in the equal exchange of goods for gold, or gold for goods.

Through Plato we know that Socrates strongly believed that every man must look to himself and seek wisdom before dealing with the external world. However, in asserting that each person seeks his own good, but he can be mistaken or ignorant of what constitutes that good, he indicated that he did not adhere to his own advice. Firstly he ought to have defined what he meant by good; and since it is; everything which is in one's own interest, nobody can consciously be ignorant as to what is in their own interest at any one time. They may well not have the wisdom or the knowledge to perform the most beneficial action, in the objective appraisal of another; but they themselves will always act in their own best interests, regardless of the certainty of another that their reasoning is defective. As it may well be; but they do not have the facility to realise it.

So the good for any one person at any one time is that which they consider it to be, and not that which is in the mind of another. No one can understand the motivations of another without fully understanding their own motivations. If Socrates makes the assessment that another's actions are mistaken all he is doing is indicating that his mind is constituted differently from the doer. All he is saying is that if he were in precisely the same circumstances as the other, then he would act differently But no two minds are alike.

Philosophers have long agonised over the essence of mind. But, in some parts of Britain people are heard to use the phrase;

'He was not minded to do it.' And therein, we are afforded as much information about mind as we can get from weeks of study of some long and dreary book on the topic. If somebody is not minded to do something then, the brain in collaboration with the psychological profile, together with accumulated experience up to that point, prevented the person from carrying out the action. I have said that nobody is consciously ignorant as to what is in their own interests. However, some do take actions which are decidedly against their own best interests. And Freud has elucidated the reasons as to why this may happen. His rationale for such occurrences is that the power of the subconscious has won the battle over the conscious. Emotional abuse in childhood lead to negative feelings about the self, being buried in the subconscious. Those lead to such feelings of worthlessness and low self-esteem that whatever the conscious tries to do in the individuals self-interest, the subconscious ruthlessly undermines the efforts, in order to keep the individual's status in an appropriate condition in accordance with its powerful feelings of worthlessness. That small piece of circuitry with its strands from the lower module to the upper module were distorted in childhood, leading to the full range of compulsive disorders and other self-destructive behaviour.

So Socrates in believing that he and others were the best judges of the most propitious kind of behaviour for other citizens, was led to the belief that the State was the fountain of justice and rectitude and the individual citizen was merely to accept it. However, the machinery of any State is not an inanimate object. And those individuals who are involved in the function of the machinery of State are no less or more defective than any other citizen. However, Socrates did not deviate much from his own reality and made an honest quest for truth.

However, the same is not entirely true for Plato. Having given the world of philosophy the exalted process of the dialectic, it was a method he himself was wont to use. He found he could readily accept the view of Heraclitus, that everything in the universe was in a state of flux; and also the view of Parmenides that everything is a changeless reality. Hence he concluded that we can have no knowledge of objects; but merely an opinion of them. He abstracted the characteristics from objects which owned them, and elevated them to a separate realm. This led to his establishment of the independent being of universals or what he termed ideas. These ideas or forms constituted reality.

In good governance he saw fit to divide the population into three classes. This number of classes was derived from his division of the soul of man into the rational, spirited and appetitive. The concept of soul, it would appear, did not face the rigours of the dialectic. He had a priori knowledge of the soul. Justice in the State was to be found in the principle that each class would perform its own duties without seeking to usurp the roles of the other classes. The State was to be run in such a way as to exclude the possibility of the desire for change arising in anyone's mind. As reason was the unquestioned master in the soul, so the class which embodies the reasoning faculty should be the governing class in the State. The implication being that the subservient class and military class was incapable of reasoning. The governing class was to receive a special education in philosophy; the purpose of which was to gain a knowledge of reality. And it was the collection of forms that constituted reality. We would have to ask here if he had more than one idea of reality in his mind. The highest good life was appropriate to the guardian class.

He also maintained that sensible objects; those which were known by means of the senses, fluctuate between the possession of qualities and the possession of the opposite qualities. Even though individual persons are known by means of the senses; this belief did not extend to members of the subservient class who were recognised as rigidly belonging to one group. And probably more importantly, he did not recognise that those in the guardian class, who may set out appearing to be enlightened benefactors could become despotic tyrants.

On his belief that objects were not anything at all, because they were always in the process of becoming something else, he ought to have recalled that Athenians did not set out to build ships for their highly efficient fleet, with the constant fear that half way through their build, the ships would become something else. Fishermen did not go out to bring back their catches in the fear that the fish would become something else prior to their return. And at thirty years of age, when Plato's relatives were influentially involved in giving Socrates the choice of being killed or killing himself, he was quite sure that the hemlock was not going to become honey soon after being swallowed. If philosophy had concerned itself with that which was relevant to man in the here and now, and pertinent to his daily life, it may not have attracted the cynicism it has.

Plato seems to have been responsible for the not entirely harmless preoccupation of some people with the idea of class. However, more negatively, he was responsible for opening the door, which permitted philosophy's decent into metaphysics. He maintained that the highest virtue was not only in having the right opinions about what was 'good' but in understanding why what was considered good was good. He did not devote himself to this aspiration. For if he had arrived at an accurate and irrefutable definition of 'good' then Aristotle would not have asserted all of what he did, and the world would, in all likelihood, be a different place today.

Aristotle disputed a great deal of what Plato asserted and believed that form and matter were the inseparable constituents of all existing things. All objects could be analysed into two constituents. Firstly the matter of which it is composed, and secondly the law of organisation or structure which accounts for its having the characteristics it has. The latter he called Form. He introduced the idea of a singular God which he conceived to be solely a law of organisation or structure. His philosophy tended to emphasise the teleological aspect of growth or the ends towards which things were seeking to evolve. And it was to resolve this question that he introduced the concept of the Deity. This was his answer to the why of the potentiality towards actuality, - or the acorn to the oak. God was seen as the magnet drawing the potential towards the actual. He did not conceive him as being creative or supervisory. He was not responsible for the world, and nor does he intervene in it. God was seen as the changeless source of value, perfect and aloof, not contaminated by interest in, or responsibility for the imperfect.

This shadow-God, he later made real, in his writings on ethics. His theism was woven into Christian beliefs in such a way as to make it indistinguishable from their own theology. The scholasticism of the medieval era was an attempt by some to authenticate a faith by aligning it with something they perceived to be based on reason.

There have been many theistic philosophers in the history of philosophy and they deserve the same approbation and applause as the tightrope walker. But the tightrope walker, who is never more than a chair's height above solid ground. Each time they encounter a difficulty, they haul in the ever reliable theistic crutch, just as the tightrope walker about to fall, puts one foot on the ground, steadies himself, and carries on as if nothing had happened. Hence it is all the more a pleasant relief when we find some who even though immersed in theistic belief are capable of distinguishing between faith and reason.

One such person was John Duns Scotus (1265-1308). He asserted that the will; commonly regarded as the pursuit of natural instincts, was that which commanded the intellect and was the source of all motivation. He held that even if the intellect was the cause of volition it is a subservient cause to the will. Thus the individual was seen as someone who was legitimately striving towards the fulfilment of the propensities of their nature, and therefore incapable of altruism. And while being aware of this truth, he was able to infer that there had to be a common nature applicable to all individuals. But when we add to this, his belief that love is superior to knowledge, we have to recognise that along with Hume, a tiny area in south east Scotland produced two of the greatest minds in philosophy.

If philosophy is to have any legitimate pursuit, it is towards an understanding of human nature, which can be found to be empirically evident. Even though Machiavelli may have had a more jaundiced view than most, his observations were no less legitimate. He observed that in general men were fickle; liars and deceivers and greedy for their own profit. Men will lie and deceive and change allegiance if it is in their own self-interest to

27

do so. But as Machiavelli was greedy for his own profit so too would he lie and deceive if it was in his own interest to do so. He observed that men would more readily do an injury to one who makes himself loved, than to one who makes himself feared. Again there is no surprise in this. A man who had made himself loved would in all likelihood be less likely to resort to violent retaliation; than one who had made himself feared. It also has to be noted that no person would do any injury to either one, if no perceivable gain could be envisaged. He also believed that the generality of his kin were simple and easily deceived.

But five hundred years after Machiavelli, people continue to demonstrate, in their support for a failed ideology, that they are easily deceived. The extension of the franchise to all adults may well be regarded in some quarters as a highly desirable factor in civilised society. However, the enthusiasm the protagonists showed in this struggle has not been matched by the majority of those whom they have liberated to vote. Many do not give any serious thought to politics. Many are more concerned with a ten second dialogue between two actors on some popular television programme than they are about politics.

Many look around and see the growing extent of irresponsible behaviour and do not consider it a political matter. At election time they will ask one question of themselves; "Will I be better off with one party or another?" And having made their choice they will vote accordingly. There can be no criticism of this reasoning since it is consistent with the natural order, and everyone who has ever voted has reasoned thus. However, being financially better off to the extent that it is insufficient to pay for the cost of buying extra security, is not being better off. People who do not think about politics do not consider social degeneration has anything to do with their vote. If the nature of man had been understood this situation could not persist.

It is regrettable that in the history of thought the utterances of some which were authentic and wise were degenerated by further utterances which were not defensible or wise. One such was Thomas Hobbes (1588-1679). His determination to transpose Galileo's mathematical methods onto the study of human activities brought his other belief's into disrepute. Having felt that everything could be explained in terms of matter in motion, he had to contend with the reality of it not being perceived as such. He felt that sensory experience resulted from the pressing on our sense organs of the motions of the matter touched or tasted. He extended this concept of pressure mediatedly to seeing, smelling and hearing.

We may be aware with the benefit of scientific investigation and discovery that our seeing an object in daylight is a result of a continuous bombardment of electromagnetic waves differentiated according to the nature of the object, and reflected back reaching an assembly of molecules in the eye we call the retina. We may also be aware that our other senses are explained in physico-chemical terms; however Hobbes' attempts to move away from the earlier metaphysical meanderings was a necessary and laudable endeavour.

In his appraisal of human nature he moved away from the strictures of the matter in motion, model. He felt that information about passions and feelings could not be deduced from information about movement of matter. He considered pleasure and pain as that which was judged as good or bad. And regarding those two concepts, he saw that that which was loved was that which was desired, and seen as good. And that which caused aversion was hated, and seen as bad. For someone who defined pity as; grief for the calamity of another, arising from the imagination, that the like calamity may befall himself; it is somewhat surprising he held the view he did on the nature of good and evil.

He did not see the natural human being as either good or evil. Then if a man slays his neighbours to steal their livestock, he would not readily empathise with the victims and regard the killer as evil. But having understood the source of empathy he would certainly have regarded the killer as evil. He saw that there was no evil in nature, and since he saw man as part of nature, he saw him as being without evil. But being without evil and being capable of carrying out deeds which would be judged as evil by another, is a very different matter. The act of judgement made the act evil, for the killer would have rationalised his behaviour and not believed himself to be evil as he carried out his deed. Hobbes may well have felt that the killer was no more inherently evil than the cheetah that kills the young deer. But for someone who stressed the importance of the preservation of life for all the citizens of the state, and the establishment of perpetual peace, he could not have held the view other than that the taking of a life was evil. He argued that the sovereign power must be authorised to have the ability great enough to restrain, through its threat of greater punishment the natural bellicose tendencies of its citizens.

One of the most important observations made by Hobbes was with regard to conflict. Even though he was writing at a time of great social unrest and instability, his remarks are as true now as they were five thousand years earlier. The natural state of man is that of someone in pursuit of his needs and wants. And in this pursuit he encounters others similarly engaged. Their needs and wants are, to all intents and purposes identical. This causes conflict and competition.

People are generally governed by the twin factors to varying degrees, of desire and fear. Before the advent of money our ancestors were driven by the desire to pursue their own self-interest; and the fear that their produce or livestock would be stolen, in yet another raid, by another tribe or settlement. Conflict and competition for resources has remained. If you, dear reader, have any money in your possession right now, the only reason; yes, the only reason, it is of any use to you, is that other people want it. If nobody else had any use for it, then it would be of no use to you. Therefore, we are all in competition with each other. The obverse of this life coin is often quoted: we need each other. That is true. But if the reverse of the life coin is not understood there will be no understanding of human nature.

At one and the same time and with equal strength; we both need each other, and are in competition with each other. This is just one of the facts that makes socialism a dishonest ideology. In that it intervenes to remove money from one citizen to give to another when they are both in competition with each other. He also spoke of the 'felicity of this life' being embodied in the continual success in obtaining our desires. But less than three hundred years after his death there came about a situation in his country where the State provided for all the desires of millions of its citizens, with money taken by force from the rest. And no feeling of success would have been apprehended by the recipients.

It is extraordinary that Hobbes, given his understanding of

the commonality of mankind, that he did not elevate the promotion of democracy in the generation of his Commonwealth. For there can be nothing more in keeping with the natural law, and the legitimate pursuit of every individual of their own self-interest, than democracy. It would have provided for the removal of the Commonwealth if it failed to uphold the natural laws which were derived from reason; or enacted artificial laws, derived from an unnatural ideology. The only possible explanation for Hobbes' omission of any mechanism for the derivation or dissolution of his Commonwealth was in his belief in the 'sanctity of right', which automatically followed from reason and the natural law; and since all men were part of the natural law, there would be no cause for rebellion against it.

He observed that the desire to preserve one's life was also a desire for peace. However, he did not impose his understanding of the essence of empathy in this equation. He contended that natural human reason recognises that peace is the desirable condition for the preservation of life. However, it is not the circumstance of peace that leads to the preservation of life, but the individual's feeling that; if I believe I have a right to life, then through empathy, I confer that right onto others. If all individuals are capable of this empathy then there will be peace. The individuals' empathy is the forerunner of peace. By the same token, if an individual feels he has the right to pursue his own interests without obstruction, interference or the infringement of his natural right by another, then he will through empathy, confer that right on others. And it is because not everybody is minded to exercise this empathy; that Hobbes believed his Commonwealth was essential; and we believe, there has to be a machinery for the preservation of law and order in every society.

In all discussions on law and the violation of law the issue of determinism is introduced to the debate. Hobbes felt that everything that takes place is causally necessitated. He also believed that there are times when we are free and times when we are not. Let us picture Hobbes who has just left his home to buy some provisions. On his way he happens upon a violent skirmish between Royalists and Roundheads. Should he continue, and be identified as supporting one side or the other, and be attacked? Or should he continue and be identified as neither supporting one side or the other, and still be attacked: or should he continue in the hope of being ignored as a disinterested passer-by? Or should he try to mediate between the two groups and rationalise that the issue was not worth the shedding of one drop of blood. He is faced with choices. He will choose the one based on all his sense experiences, on all his analytical thought, on all his acquired wisdom in assessing the demeanour of his fellow man up to that time. He almost instantly chooses; that discretion being the better part of valour, to turn around and go back home. He was not free to continue in the pursuit of his requirements but he was free to make the choice of waiting for another day.

The cause of this behaviour was the motivation to act in his own self-interest and in that respect he was not free from causal necessity. Since given everything that made him the man he was at that point, he had to make. that decision. The logical determinists would argue that all of his experiences up to that point played no part in his wish to act in his own best interest. They can hold that view; but it affords us nothing, in an attempt to gain insight into human nature. The idea Hobbes had of; from whence the power ought to be derived, to provide the power to protect the lives and preserve the property and rights of all citizens, was more important to him than the eventual structure itself. And that idea was derived from the understanding of an important aspect of human nature. That we are motivated perpetually by our own self-interest. Curiously the man who chose to dispute Hobbes' thinking, differed from him in only the slightest degree.

That being, Joseph Butler (1692-1752). If some of the aspects of both men's thinking could have been combined somehow, it would have provided a formidable understanding of human nature. While in Hobbes' understanding of pity, he had glimpsed the importance of empathy, Butler was keenly aware of the importance of self-love. He argued that self-love included benevolence towards others. But not only is this true, but there will only be benevolence towards others, if self-love is a predominant factor in the make up of the individual. He saw fit to consider appetites, passions, affections, and the ability to make judgements as being at the lowest level of a hierarchy of human nature. Ascending to Benevolence, Self-love and Conscience at the highest level. He believed it was in no way necessary to neglect one's own interest and pleasure to behave virtuously. Not only was this not the case but since benevolence and self-love were so perfectly coincident, that the greatest satisfaction to ourselves is derived from exhibiting benevolence in due degree. But it was with his idea of conscience where he could be accused of the same circularity as Aristotle, with his idea of good. He saw conscience as that which pronounced to each individual in their daily lives that which was right and wrong. And this would happen if the hierarchy of principles was functioning in its natural order.

However, he must have observed the behaviour of persons in his life which indicated to him that their hierarchy of principles

34

was disordered. He made no suggestion as to why this hierarchy would go awry. If conscience was the governor of the appetites, affections and passions, then why did it not govern one person in like manner to all the rest. He saw that conscience was the spring from which primary and fundamental laws of all civil constitutions of all nations flowed. He saw that this conscience gave rise to the practise of justice, veracity and regard for the common good. But Hobbes would not have disagreed with this. He would have equated Butler's conscience with his own enlightened self-interest.

Not having identified the source and the essence of the idea of conscience he would always face difficulties with the idea. His contemporary the Earl of Shaftesbury considered that his fellow man had an, instinct for benevolence, but he did not recognise any ruling conscience in human nature. He also; would have looked around him and observed that this instinct for benevolence varied widely from one person to the next, but made no offer of suggestion as to why this might be.

Hobbes had contended that our apparently benevolent or compassionate actions are performed in order to acquire friends, appease enemies or gain some other advantage. Butler contested this, with the question as to how we derive pleasure from the fact that someone else may alleviate another's misfortune. If he had noted Hobbes definition of pity he may have been able to answer this. We derive pleasure because through empathy we conduct an immediate ego transference and visualise ourselves in the situation of the recipient of the benefit. Hobbes was not entirely correct to speak of, apparent benevolence or compassionate behaviour. These are not necessarily apparent. They can be real and the pay-off is; the assuaging of the psyche through empathy;

even though there may be other pay-offs on other occasions or no other pay-off. Similarly, Butler questioned our discrimination with regard to our preparedness to be good to one person and not another. Again we will assist one and not another depending on the degree to which we empathise with one or the other. Being the Bishop of Durham, Butler, like Scotus, deserves the greatest acclamation for moving away from revealed religion in his attempt to gain insight into human nature.

Another who tried to define how the individual could be accommodated appropriately within the sovereign State, and remain free, was Jack Rousseau (1712-1778). He is probably best known for his remark "Man is born free and everywhere he is in chains". However, neither part of this statement is true. Man is born with a series of needs, which he sets out to satisfy as he journeys through life. The necessary endeavour which this task generates thus creates many constraints and compulsions but, saving slavery: no chains. Even though his use of the word would have been meant metaphorically, chains are never externally imposed. Man's metaphorical chains are only those he is prepared to contribute towards making himself. He rightly asserted that law sets people free. In every society there will be some individuals who will seek to impose their will on others, in varying degrees of viciousness. The structure of law, which ought to be derived from natural law, is there to provide protection against such behaviour.

He also believed that if each citizen was adequately informed and deliberated rationally then the sovereign government would be right. Sadly when that ideal state of affairs does not exist, the government we get will try to pursue a failed ideology at enormous expense to most citizens. In his structure;

the sovereign government would be a direct reflection of the citizens in association. Then somewhat schizophrenically he questions the useful involvement of individual citizens in the generation of the sovereign government. He asks;

"How can a blind multitude which often does not know what it wills, because it rarely knows what is good for it, carry out for itself so great and difficult an enterprise as a system of legislation?"

This question could be used by any autocratic dictator to justify their existence. A mistake often made by people who do not appreciate the diverse individuality of any perceived group is to confine them to groups such as, a blind multitude, or the rich, or the poor.

Within any imagined grouping or class there will be those who are aspiring towards a better life for themselves, and others who will engage in such behaviour that will mitigate their progress towards a better life. And within those changing groups some life event will inspire others to arrest a downward spiral, and progress, towards a better life. While others, may regress temporarily or continually. If life, and human nature is not understood from the perspective of the individual, it will not be understood at all. Even though Rousseau demonstrates a high regard for personal freedom; in other utterances he elevates the sovereign power above the citizen. He feels that the association between sovereign and citizen would work if every individual gives up their rights.

But in every form of government under natural law, the government ought to be the servant of the people; not the people the servants of the government. The citizens would pay their taxes to employ the government to carry out for them certain functions which individuals could not practically provide for themselves on an individual basis. Some of the more important are; a maintenance of law and order, a defence capability and expenditure on infrastructure. Even though Rousseau borrowed heavily from Hobbes, he missed the most important aspect of Hobbes' thinking. That the structure of government would evolve because it was in the self-interest of every individual that it would. And no rights that any individual felt they had, under natural law, prior to the establishment of that government, would need to be relinquished.

Another who looked about his world and considered the prevailing conditions somewhat wanting was Jeremy Bentham (1748-1832). He felt that the only justified object of all legislation was to secure the greatest happiness for the greatest number. It has to be said firstly that, this intonates that he was in a position to know what constituted that happiness, and secondly, that this law was going to originate from 'on high'; in his head, and disseminate down to the citizen. This utilitarian doctrine needed to utilise a, 'felicific calculus', to calculate the quantity of happiness which was likely to result from given actions. In order to assist in this he identified seven properties that were pertinent to pain and pleasure. Those being: intensity, duration, certainty, propinquity, fecundity, purity, and extent. He did appreciate that applying this to the great variety of individuals with their individual idiosyncrasies and predilections was somewhat problematic. But one of the more important things he observed was that each person is psychologically predisposed to seek his or her own happiness. But he felt that this would be tempered by a morality that would require one to act in such a way as to bring about the greatest good for everyone. But he had contended that happiness was the supreme moral value. Therefore the pursuit of happiness was tempered by happiness. Even though this may not be entirely illogical; for a man who had something of a legal reputation, words such as morality, pleasure and happiness, which do not mean the same thing to any two individuals must have left him with considerable unease.

Later, J.S. Mill (1806-1873) found himself having to defend the accusations by the critics of utilitarianism that it represented humankind as selfish and base. The first of these is merely a truism. But it was the interchangeability of the words pleasure and happiness that led to the belief that everybody, only, pursued their own pleasure and, that pleasure was the greatest good. Then if the ingredient of legislation is added; the object of which was to give rise to this circumstance, it is not difficult to see why criticism was attracted. Mill then tried to identify actions which he perceived not to be selfish, and sought to derive formulae for the utilitarian doctrine. Those two formulae were centred on act-utilitarianism and rule-utilitarianism. The former was based on the necessary reflection by the individual prior to some action, as to what was going to produce the greatest happiness. The latter was to be derived from the resolution of the former and was to become a rule applicable in future. However, no individual's life is broken up into stop-go segments as is implied by this method. On his beliefs regarding universal causality he came to describe a cause as;

"the sum total of the conditions, positive and negative taken together; the whole of the contingencies of every description which being realised, the consequent action inevitably follows".

This may well suffice as the definition of a cause; but then it suffices for the causes of all actions. He looked around, and he saw war and interpersonal violence and he saw no happiness or pleasure derived by either party, even though those actions had the same cause as others, where happiness and pleasure may be perceived to have ensued. The accusation that their beliefs portrayed humankind as base, was because their doctrine implied generality. Individual human beings had produced great inventions, great works of art, great architecture and none could be considered base. But those individuals were motivated not by consideration of the greatest happiness for the greatest number, but by consideration of their own benefit and aggrandisement. If their works produced an improvement in the quality of life of the many; then the many was a derivative of the success sought by the original motivation. The kind of legislation the utilitarians appeared to seek was such that it would only have been consistent with the thinking of the average Benthamite, and the rest of humankind would fall outside its remit.

On considering the utilitarian's precept one cannot help imagining; a rotund man standing behind a great crock doling out spoonfuls of jam to awaiting mouths, and when the crock was empty, those at the back were just unfortunate to miss out.

The pragmatists, had they been contemporaries would have been able to clarify some of the utilitarian's thought. Especially C.S. Peirce (1839-1914) who had his own view on rules of action. More properly, he saw that the assuaging of doubt through thought, after a sufficient number of experiences, would result in beliefs which would produce habits, or rules of action. And the rule of action would reveal the strength of the belief from which it derived. So somebody like Mill, who may have been considering an affair with a married woman would have considered it judicious to ascertain how much unhappiness it would cause to the woman's husband, before proceeding in pursuit of his own happiness. Only then would he have been able to have the belief to proceed with his action.

Peirce asserted that our habits of action are acquired through the connections thought makes between feelings and actions. And I contend that feelings take their design from the psychological profile of the individual. Then, neurological activity in the brain, in connection with the psychological profile motivates all actions. In being rightly suspicious of the idealists he asserted that:

"our idea of anything is our idea of its sensible effects, and if we conceive we have any other we deceive ourselves."

His successor William James (1842-1910) would have provided further clarity when he contended that individual human beings are part of a natural system, within which we are continually reshaping our activities and strategies in response to everything we encounter. He rightly asserted that it is experience; rather than theory, abstractions and metaphysical philosophy, that is the key to a practical understanding of ourselves and the world we live in.

He maintained that the mind had to be seen as the instrument for realising purposes. And that the primary function of thought was to enable us to relate to the world and the people around us. That its purpose is to, "carry us prosperously from any one part of our experience to any other part". And that the truth of any theory or belief can be ascertained if living by them produces 'satisfactory relations with other parts of our experience'. True ideas are those we can assimilate, validate and corroborate. And accordingly he turned the spotlight on those in philosophy who alleged to have a concept of a substance composing an underlying reality, that supported the perceived world. He felt that since this had no bearing on the real world, it made no practical difference to anyone's life. Their view merely highlighted the poverty of much philosophical speculation.

He did see fit however to make a distinction between the 'I' and the 'me'. But this is merely linguistic convenience. No individual is ever conscious of a separate notion of 'I' and 'me'. He also studied the differences between the type of temperament that was more likely to be a rationalist or empiricist. But the only thing that had philosophical relevance was how much verifiable truth any of them contributed.

Another who indicated that he recognised the importance of individual experience was Soren Kierkegaard (1813-1855), when he said;

"The thinker who can forget in all his thinking also to think that he is an existing individual will never explain life."

He saw that such a thinker merely seeks to cease to be a human being. But more important to the message herein was his belief that the individual human will, and the fact of choice are of supreme importance. And those who saw human beings as merely elements in an inevitable process were not only philosophically mistaken, but were promoting an abdication of responsibility. He saw that the making of choices displayed a recognition of one's complete individual separateness and responsibility for oneself. And in this activity the individual achieved an ethical reality which ought to mean more to them than heaven and earth and all that is therein.

Just as Kierkegaard saw fit to question some predecessors view of reality, G.E. Moore (1873-1958) saw fit to suggest that philosophical problems exist because of what some philosophers have said about the world of the sciences. His beliefs suggested a move from idealism to commonsenseism. He held that the most valuable thing we can know or imagine is, the state of consciousness, which may be roughly described as the pleasures of human intercourse and the enjoyment of beautiful objects. He believed that the greatest good is that of personal affection. And he questioned the belief of some who held that good belonged solely to a Perfect Being. This would then preclude the possibility of any human endeavour making an impact on the condition.

But it was in respect of the idea of 'good' that Moore demonstrated no more insight than many others. Having contended that good was indefinable and unanalysable he still saw that it is possible to identify certain things as pre-eminently good. Then one wonders why he did not ponder on how he could make this judgement on those certain things. If personal affection and aesthetic enjoyments were good, then what was it about them that made them good?

Because mankind is faced with the task of providing for their own needs to ensure their own survival, a stress response results in each individual. This in turn causes a certain state of nervous arousal. As soon as a human being becomes involved in either of the activities which Moore described as good, this level of nervous arousal starts to decrease. It decreases because the individual is free from involvement in the necessary efforts of survival. The slowing down of the breathing; and the reduction of heart rate and blood pressure causes a relaxation response. This; to the human animal feels good. And as Peirce pointed out, after successive similar experiences, the belief is formed that this behaviour is good, and a habit is formed. Hence neither of the two activities, lose their desirability, or go out of fashion for human beings. Moore did not have to be aware of the autonomic nervous system and its division into the sympathetic and parasympathetic which followed a few decades later from Hans Selye's work; but he was mindful that the activities he mentioned were desirable. And it was because he found them desirable, he called them good. One wonders why this was not manifestly obvious.

Even further away from a definition of good was Wittgenstein, who felt that all utterances about good and bad were unsayable. And consequently felt it was impossible for there to be propositions of ethics. However, for someone who said: "It is clear that we need a foothold for the will in the world", he seems to have accepted that without this foothold, neither 'good nor a system of ethics could be defined or proposed. He was dismissive about the benefits of philosophy up to his time, and may have provided a clue as to the reasons for this paucity of truth. In his remark about philosophers and 'our craving for generality' he has pinpointed the chief obstacle to truth. Those who try to infer what is in the minds of the many, without knowing what is in their own mind.

If Moritz Schlick (1882-1936) had followed through on his proper determination to distinguish between, an investigation into what the norms of conduct are, and an investigation into the causes of their being what they are, he may have gleaned some truths. For to investigate the causes of his own conduct he would have to question himself. He considered the pursuit of knowledge in this area to be the proper task of ethics. And he recognised that if the problem of ethics was in the causal explanation of behaviour, then the method of discovery was psychological. In order to arrive at truth, he maintained a verification principle which stated that: the meaning of a principle is the method of its verification. And we can come to understand the meaning of a statement if we know what kind of observations verify it. More importantly for all those interested in truth he declared that when there is no method of verification for a statement, the statement has no meaning. Like any sensible gardener who understands that flowers will not grow up if weeds are there to choke them, Schlick understood that the flowers of truth would not grow if weeds were there to choke them. And those overgrown weeds were the weeds of metaphysics.

4. The Dishonest Detractors

None of the philosophers so far mentioned have given any cause for suspicion that they were not honestly engaged in the pursuit of truth. As Plato who did not have the insight to dispense with either the view of Heraclitus or Parmenides, or both, seems to have believed that there was some merit in each. Aristotle saw that form did not exist without matter, yet was able to say that God was not composed of matter, but did exist in form . If we want to know why a thing has become what it has, he argued, we can observe it through stages, of material cause, formal cause, efficient cause and final cause. This explanation did not extend to God, which he saw as detached, not creative or supervisory, not responsible for, and non-interfering in the world. Simply a thing which drew the potential towards the actual.

However, in his ethics, some strange anthropomorphic belief had crept in, having been given no critical discourse. He equates him with, the reasoning faculty, with the supreme good, and confers on him the enjoying of some simple pleasure, and being for ever in contemplation. Whatever Aristotle's exact ideas were on any issue we ought to be mindful of the fact that he was one of a succession of Greek thinkers which had started with perhaps the greatest of them all Anaximander. And a writer whose works somehow precariously survived ought to generate no more reverence in anyone, than any other writer, if their utterances do not find resonance with their own experiences. However, pioneers in objective thought are a very different matter from those, who two thousand years later, set out to deceive. One of these was Emmanuel Kaut (1724-1804). He set out, not to derive any truths, but to philosophise in futility. He was convinced, perhaps not unreasonably, that if people were impressed by Aristotle and Plato then they would be impressed by him.

Having concluded that there was no necessary reason why the human mind should be an instrument capable of discovering the truth about the universe he set out in pursuit of what knowledge if anything could he incontrovertibly accepted. He saw that the human mind worked in accordance with certain prescribed laws of mathematics, logic and reasoning. But, he contested; those laws may be laws about the workings of the mind and not in any sense laws about the material world. How do we know, he asked, that these laws of thought really apply to things? And unless we do know this we have no guarantee that our knowledge will give us truth about reality.

He concluded that our knowledge of the external world is limited and conditioned by the limits and conditions of our own minds. We obtain knowledge not of reality but of appearances. The reality which lies behind those appearances is, and must remain unknown. The appearance of something which is available to our senses he called; phenomenon.

A phenomenon therefore, is anything that we know which has been contaminated by our act of knowing. He stressed that the perception of an object was an active experience. The mind acts as a lawgiver to nature, prescribing to the world we know the forms and conditions under which it is perceived. And how did our mind happen to have those forms and conditions? He answered that we never really observe and experience; we always go out beyond what we observe and contribute to it. And how do we do this? Through what we already know. And we already know this as it is the mind a priori. Therefore, independent of any sense experience of an object we can know the object. And this comes about by pure forms of intuition. Matter is what is given in sensation but we have to think of form as being 'in the mind'.

He tells us we do not see what we see, but that the knowledge we have is founded on subjective experiences which are produced by external entities that act on the senses. And he termed; the minds assessment and embroidering of what it sees, as synthetic a priori judgements.

He conceived the mind as being initially fitted with a number of mental apparatus, the peculiarities of which were imposed on everything that it knew. Some of which were the apparatus of space, time, quantity and quality. So those 'categories', as he termed them, interposed themselves between reality and our minds, thus preventing us from ever knowing reality. The reality which we could never know, or that world which was uninterpreted by our knowledge, he termed; noumena.

The Universe then he divided into two realms, the real or the noumenal and the apparent or phenomenal. He termed objects in the noumenal world, transcendental objects. And the individual Self when acting morally, the transcendental Self.

He maintained that when we will and act morally we are in direct touch with reality and therefore in the noumenal world. Moral actions are those which proceed from a good will. Morality is the name that he gives to actions of which his society approves, and his own actions are determined by his desire to be of good standing with his fellows and by fear of their disapproval. So his view of morality was formed not by him, but for him, by others. The feeling of moral obligation is something he cannot account for in phenomenal terms. From the point of view of anthropology men act according to inclination; they do what they like, and avoid what they don't like, their actions are what he calls 'heteronomous', governed by laws over which they have no control.

But there is a further judgement which men make - a moral judgement – which guides them not in their wants; but in what they ought to do. Thus the claim of morality cuts right across the pull of inclination and desire. Hence anthropologically man is not free, but morally he acts and considers as if he were free. The moral self escapes the determinist and phenomenal world into the noumenal world. He called the obligation to act morally, 'The Categorical Imperative', the commands of which were absolute and unqualified. He claims that moral judgements are completely unaffected by circumstances and no consideration is taken of possible consequences.

He concedes that some may act usually or even always as non-moral beings but insists the moral will is always present. He accepts that some people act wrongly in order to benefit themselves in some way but he saw no motivation for truth telling or acting honestly. These were engaged in for their own sake. In so far as we act in accordance with desire we are not free, it is only when we act morally that we are free. This obedience to the moral law is something, which he considered, could not be explained. He perceived that our moral obligation expresses a sort of necessity which occurs nowhere else in nature. And was also able to say that we never have experience of nature, as nature is in herself.

We really do need to remind ourselves when we observe Kant's series of pronouncements that he is the same person who set out in search of truth. Almost immediately he discovers an insurmountable obstacle to our appraisal of reality. He never found it compelling to explain how the a priori knowledge which contaminated our view of reality got to the mind in the first instance. He seems to have borrowed the idea of our having innate ideas from Descartes. His 'categories' were some kind of agile formulae that immediately jumped in between our attempted perception and reality. Even though it is clear that a vulture or a rabbit is fitted with most of his categories, he was not concerned to look out beyond the window of his lecture room in Berlin.

And in trying to drive a wedge of absolute difference between ourselves in moral experience and in non moral experience we arrive at the interpretation, that; if I desire to go to work I am not acting morally, but if I do not desire to go to work, but yet go, then I am acting morally. In his own interpretation of moral behaviour he creates contradiction. His behaving morally is motivated by his desire to be of good standing with his fellows because of fear of their disapproval. But in so far as he was acting in his own inclination and desire he was governed by laws over which he had no control. This therefore placed him in his anthropological or phenomenal world, where no moral action can take place.

If he considers that moral actions are carried out with no consideration of possible consequences then how does he explain his moral actions entered into so as to avoid the disapproval of others. Was their disapproval not a possible consequence? The fact that he considered that some actions were engaged in for their own sake demonstrated that he did not engage his own thought processes. He did not question the possible origin of moral obligation.

There are different kinds of obscurity. There is the expression of obscurity and the obscurity of expression. Kant wallowed in the latter. He uses abstract conceptions and obscure exposition, coupled with linguistic gymnastics to disguise the fact that he had nothing to offer of any value to anybody. He was, in a word, a fraud.

He set out on a make-believe epistemological escapade from a position of near darkness to arrive at a position of total darkness. He successfully bamboozled his students with meaningless phrases such as . . . activity of the understanding . . . the manifold of pure intuition . . . an affection of the mind, in order to deter them from questioning anything. He would have undoubtedly used the ploy of all inept teachers, of embarrassing the interrogator with the remark, "so you don't understand?" So he got away with it, and is still getting away with it.

On one question which he asked himself he felt no shame on relying on Aristotle's circularity as to the origin of the moral will. He answers. From the nature of man regarded as a moral being. And as if that was insufficient his view of the moral law is this. What the moral law prescribed is that we should act in every case upon general principles which are intuitively recognised to be morally binding. Intuitively recognised . . . !? Are we dealing here with someone who has been called a great philosopher or someone who has the mentality of a fairground fortune teller? The fortune teller, at least does not pretend to be other than she is, but he did pretend to be other than he was, and that is why he was a fraud. He did have cause in his writings to mention the genuinely great Scottish philosopher David Hume (1711-1777). But, philosophically Kant was not fit to clean David Hume's discarded shoes. Those who think Kant had something to offer are the same kind of highly insecure unthinking grown-ups who cash in all their worldly goods, and take the proceeds along to some fringe religious sect, whose leader puts it towards another private jet.

One person who was duly impressed and trotted along behind Kant tugging at his cassock, was Georg Hegel (1770-1831). One thing that has to be observed about the evolution of frauds is the way in which the successor looks around at the manner in which fools absorb the gibberish of the former. And they vow; that they too, could become great if they write something similar.

The true purpose of philosophy is to strive to provide an understanding of human nature and human behaviour and to accurately appraise mankind's position in the Universe.

So Hegel set out from the standpoint of mysticism, secure in the knowledge that his 'philosophy' could not be readily jettisoned by those who read it. If he could make it more abstruse than Kant's, then it would be decades, maybe centuries, before people saw it for what it was. He maintained Kant's distinction between the world of appearance and that of reality, but he conceived the world of reality differently. He felt no single thing in the world can be adequately known or properly understood when it is treated in isolation. Because of his feeling of being the exponent of an unveiled mystery he was able to say that his philosophical predecessors had mistakenly approached the whole theory of knowledge.

They had thought of the object known and the knowing mind as two different things and of knowledge a relation that connected them together. However he insisted that knowledge was initially a unity containing the two aspects of the knowing mind and the object known.

If we take the object to be a sword. We don't start with a mind or with the sword which the mind knows. We start with the act of knowledge. Knowledge of the sword is a unity within which we distinguish the two aspects, knowing mind, and, sword known. We make this distinction for our own practical purposes. They are both, mental abstractions which do not exist in reality as separate isolated things.

Hence the structure of thought, besides constituting the world of reality, contains within itself the world of appearances also. The world of appearances is a partially revealed aspect of the world of reality. If a horse appears to me, I do not know it as a horse unless I interpret it in line with his axiom of internal relations. That is, relating it to other objects internal to the one unity. I must recognise it to be bigger than a mule, smaller than an elephant, faster than a goat and less malodorous than a skunk. All these, and other relations with objects and creatures make it the horse that it is. These relations determine in part the horse's nature, and therefore partially constitute the horse. Hence the relation of all objects necessary in qualifying the horse, are similarly related to all other objects in one entire mesh of relations determining unity.

Therefore, apparent differences are illusory. Taken in abstraction things are not understandable because they are not self-sufficient and therefore not real. So thought and thing, were brought together in one coherent unified structure of thought. This is Hegel's timeless structure of thought which he termed the Absolute. And his view of reality was the unfolding of the Absolute or Spirit. This process of unfolding to a stage where, all is spirit, was a process of eliminating the irreducible otherness of what is grasped by the intellect. One of the more apposite means of comprehending the Absolute or Spirit for Hegel was the observation of romantic art. But should a lesser man beside him peer out through the window and see a blacksmith in his forge, his spiritual nature would be sullied by his intellect. As what appears to us as, other than spirit, is only spirit on a level of unconsciousness which the process of the development of spirit can eliminate.

Other things that may be grasped by the intellect are irrational ideas. And a method Hegel devised for the forward propulsion of the Spirit toward transparent knowledge, was his dialectal triad. It, would move from one position to its contradiction, and from there to a conclusion which would embody the insights contained in each stage. This synthesis would again be contradicted and so the process of clarification would go on. He saw, reason; as being at the centre of reality. And so while there are irrational forces at work within reality they belong to and fit into a rational pattern, and ultimately the rational is the real and the real the rational. His aim was to construct a unified philosophic system.

His philosophy is an attempt to make the whole of reality in all its variations and continual change rationally intelligible. This involved him in a reappraisal of the intellectual process, and conceptual equipment, normally used by philosophers to interpret reality.

He suggested that his dialectic method should be used with regard to the history of philosophy to illustrate the progressive grasping of reality that had occurred with the reintroduction of each synthesis to the new triad. He elaborated more on how the dialectic impacted on the 'march of time'.

He acknowledges all the human suffering, sadness, and despair of past history, but asserts that no intervention could have changed any aspect. When he is asked to address the aim and purpose of all bygone inhumanities within his Absolute, he replies that all endeavours, interests, and activities constitute the instruments and means of the Spirit or Absolute for attaining its object. That object being; until reason governs the world.

His monistic idealism while retaining the idea that everything that exists is in the nature of thought, abolishes the notion of the individual mind. In the act of knowledge the individual mind is transcended, and is itself then, just an aspect of the whole of knowledge.

Like Kant he had no difficulty with the concept of eternally held innate ideas. So when the child sees a sword for the first time there is no enquiring mind, no perceiving mind, there is, knowing mind. His avowed approach was a re-appraisal of the intellectual process to interpret reality. But what he did was engage in an elaborate pushing under the carpet exercise. He constructed what was in effect a sealed unity in which imperfections like irrationality had arisen. He did not suggest any reason as to why this arose, or any reason as to why it would ultimately fizzle out. Would this force for fizzling out not be continually met in his sealed Absolute with its antitheses; on equal force for the reintroduction of irrationality?

Presumably he was not the one in his garret in Stuttgart in 1800 to create this Absolute or Spirit or Unity. It must have always been there. So for what purpose was the generation of irrationality to be moved along towards extinction on the backs of the suffering of hundreds of millions of people? He alluded to how preceding philosophies fitted into his thesis – antithesis – synthesis model, towards the aim of grasping reality. But it is clear that if we recall the pronouncements of the very early Greek philosophers, and juxtapose them with Hegel's; we must be persuaded that his dialectal method had been in some kind of cataclysmic reversal.

But in a world then, as now, when most people don't think very deeply about very much, he got away with it. He was careful in his pronouncements to stay on the right side of the Prussian authorities, to stay in his job. In his remark;

"It is in the organisation of the state that the divine enters into the real."

he was able to ensure that whatever type of organisation that was, it would have his support. But then if his remark was only true, with reference to the ideal state; and that being the Prussian state, the National Socialists of the later Germany had legitimised ammunition in their march toward divinity.

While Hegel was disseminating his views to the unfortunate students he maintained a deliberately deterrent disqualifying demeanour. So if we imagine any questioning of him along the lines of; if it's possible to say that; given this, how can you arrive at that conclusion? We can feel sure that it would be followed by such a bout of coughing, throat clearing, page turning and snuff assisted response, that the stares from fellow students would have provided the unvocalised reproach of; how could you disturb the mind of such a great person with such a question? Can't you see already, how he struggles to produce complete sentences without your impertinence?

So I want to create my own sect of Hegelianism. And say that when a vehicle is parked near a building it forms a bond with the building. That is why when it wants to move away it can only do so slowly as the bond is being broken. And like carbon atoms that want to be together, vehicles always want to be close to other vehicles on roads, or car parks or forecourts. And as the vehicle moves on its journey it recognises that the speed camera is part of the vehicle, as the vehicle is part of the camera. Hence we observe a reverential slowing down by the vehicle, a kind of genuflection, as it passes the camera. And when due deference to the bond is shown the vehicle returns to its earlier speed.

The point is that if any Lutheran theologian or charlatan of any kind, wants to concoct a belief system which is divorced from observation, self knowledge or common sense reality; they can easily do so. There is no gainsaying any abstract ratiocination used to validate any mystical experience. But mystical experiences being at the opposite end of the spectrum from analytical knowledge have no place whatever in philosophy. But like Kant he got away with it, because, sadly, people are prepared to believe anything. The saddest thing is that university professors are more readily prepared to believe Hegel's hogwash than any greengrocer. The professor has a highly developed capacity to absorb and regurgitate. But that greater ability seems to cause a diminution in the alacrity to question. If educated citizens don't question that which ought to be questioned, then we can, as now, find ourselves in the grip of fraudulent socialism.

It wasn't just that Hegel's beliefs gave rise to the world war started in autumn 1939; but that his ideas were read by an undisciplined student at a Bonn university in 1837. The fact that Hegel's ideas inspired Karl Marx (1818-1883) to write his diatribe against employment providers of the day, has caused, and is still causing a great deal more suffering than that war.

Even though there was not one shred of evidence that Hegel's dialectic dynamic had the remotest scrap of authenticity, it was accepted by Marx. He retained the framework and concepts, but inverted it for his own purposes. He saw that all development whether thought or, more importantly things, is brought about through a conflict of opposing elements or tendencies. Hegel gave logical priority to thought over things. But Marx held that thought was a reflection of things. He held that there can be no such thing as disinterested thoughts; thought which is merely concerned to know, did not exist. And he considered the question as to the reality or non-reality of a thought which was isolated from practise as a purely scholastic question.

He rejected the Hegelian concept of the Absolute as a true reality and instead placed human life and human consciousness at the centre of his philosophy. And it was not human consciousness that determined their existence, but on the contrary, their social and political existence determined their consciousness. And the mode of production in material life determined the general character of the social, political and spiritual processes of life.

He believed in the necessary development of human material life and human nature towards a unity and harmony in their controlling forces. Being then focussed on a physical and material reality he identified the working-class or proletariat as the suitable catalyst towards attaining this harmony. And he selected the working-class, as he observed their utter self-alienation and profound impoverishment. And echoing Hegel's axiom of internal relations, he suggested that the productive forces such as manual labour, tools, machinery and raw material give rise to 'relations of production' between the people who deploy, and those who are deployed within the productive system.

Having substituted Hegel's thought, for the forces of production, it was this he saw as the prime mover in his dialectal process. And just as in the world of thought the pursuance of a tendency to its logical conclusion reveals its opposite, then, in the world of fact the very success of one movement tends to call into existence its opposite. He chose to believe that slave-holding, feudal and capitalist societies evolved as they were opposites of the former. And this phase of historical development of societies was to continue with the demise of capitalism.

This was to arise, he argued, because capital is always rising; the ratio of labour to capital gradually decreases. Therefore profits must diminish, and capitalism would therefore end. This crumbling away of the economic substructure because of the altered ratio was not going to bring about an end to capitalism, on its own.   Some assistance to the natural process was needed because the political, legal and moral systems which had grown up to prop up capitalism had generated a life of their own, and had the necessary vitality to persist.

The governing class and the custodians of this system, had a vested interest in clinging to their interests and privileges and would have to be parted from them in a violent struggle. The means of production and exchange was the basis of all social structure. So if that social structure was going to change it was not to be sought in men's brains, or in men's better insight into eternal truth and justice, but in the changes in the modes of production and exchange. So the manner in which things were owned and worked determined the relationship between men and men. He saw that relationship, as one of exploitation.

He hailed the fundamental fact in every capitalist society to be that, most men are only allowed to work on condition that they pay tribute to the owners of the means of production. In his view of the development of human material life towards a unity and harmony he envisaged the factory worker becoming the factory owner and the factory owner becoming the factory worker and never the two could be distinguished one from the other. But he only spoke in individual terms in so far as they were personifications of a particular class.

When his communism was established the dialectic process would cease. As no class antagonism would exist to generate the next seed of destruction of communism. It is remarkable that with both Hegel and Marx when both of their desired conditions transpired, a process that had brought them about, and had been going on for all of history was to conveniently stop.

By a simple inference; if the mode of production determined social existence and social existence determined consciousness, then the mode of production determined consciousness. Therefore since the concept of selling one's labour, or ideas such as the mode of production, were relatively recent facets of human life, one has to wonder how consciousness was available to his not so distant ancestors. Or similarly those too young to be aware of the financial rigours or the nuns and monks in their self sufficient monasteries would be devoid of consciousness.

In his belief in the necessary development of human material life and human nature towards a unity and harmony, it is not easy to see how this should result from a violent struggle. And if all development whether of thought or things was brought about through conflict of opposing elements, one has to ask, what opposing elements gave rise to the wheel, the galleon or the printing press?

By far the most illuminating aspect, not only of the weakness of his belief system, but of the nature of the man, came in his appraisal of the position of things. In asserting that things inspire thought, he is acknowledging that he is a victim of things. He saw himself as a tiny twig being swept along by a river rendering him, powerless and helpless. His indiscipline and parasitism revealed a person who could not conceive of having any control of his life. It is the same defeatist attitude that pervades the disciples of socialism. He felt less able to act on his environment than a blackbird, a squirrel, or a beaver.

The oft uttered statement, as if it were fact, of the pursuance of a tendency to its logical conclusion revealing its opposite, is no more true than, snow tending toward fire, or granite toward jelly, or indeed 'good' toward 'bad'. There can be no doubt that in the same way as he empathised with the profoundly impoverished working-class, as he was impoverished himself, his enmity for the State derived from his knowledge that three States had issued warrants for his arrest forcing him to stay in London.

His puerile rationale for the demise of capitalism almost beggars belief, in light of the fact that nearly every major European city had been increasing its population by up to fifty percent over six decades from the early fifteen hundreds.

In trying to stay with Hegel's thinking he asserted that as knowing is the preliminary to action, matter is its opportunity. And he saw matter as the raw material which is known in order that it may be transformed by the knowing worker into a completed product. But he himself was pathologically immersed in the avoidance of such activity.

He had asserted that the final causes of all social changes are to be sought not, in men's brains or in men's better insight, but in changes in the modes of production and exchange. But if that was his proviso, how did he envisage change happening? Was it going to be tidal wave, earthquake or meteorological conditions? Individual men effect change due to their artifice, improved techniques or invention. And they are thus motivated in the knowledge that the use of their brains would result in gain for them. If there was no prospect of gain there would be no motivation to change.

It was the manner in which things were owned and worked,

he felt, that determined the relationship between men and men. But in this he revealed the same kind of myopia as Hegel. He would have been better giving some consideration to the fact that there were no factory owners in the not so distant past. He would have been better off considering why some men become factory owners and others factory workers. Or far more appropriately; why some men shrink most determinedly from either position. Many men in history may have been pathologically indolent but they did not sit down and write the longest excuse and justification in history for that indolence.

Some people have commented that he was not concerned about his writing being regarded as a philosophy. But he knew he had played the same trick as Hegel had with Kant. If his writing had solely been a political or economic system with no reference to any metaphysical malady, then it would have been ignored. But he knew it would gain credibility on the back of the gullibility of those who had applauded Hegel's hogwash.

He had no compunction in asserting that up to his time, philosophies had only interpreted the world, but the real task was to alter it. It is curious therefore that a man had designs on altering the world, but he was not motivated to alter the fact that his own children were starving to death before his eyes. Reptiles, racoons and rats diligently care for their young. But he had no such inclination. He was a man consumed by jealousy and greed who wanted to devise a system of legalised theft so that he could have all his wants provided for him by others.

In the unity he proposed; the parasitical individual would quite conveniently not be noticed. Those who are consumed by jealousy and greed are capable of being violent to those whom they perceive as having more than themselves. And hence, his recommendation of the violent struggle. He wanted to take the waiting out of wanting; the same smash and grab mentality as the present day mugger. Marx was full of hate. He would have been better off reading the importance of enlightened self-love by Joseph Butler than the metaphysical chicanery of Hegel.

No human being who has self love is capable of hating or mugging another. No human being who has self love is capable of despising another. But socialism, this dilute communism, can only come into being and prosper because some human beings despise others. It is when we truly understand human nature that we can see so clearly, the fraudulent nature of socialism.

In Britain, the Marxist maxim, 'from each according to their ability, to each according to their need,' is alive, and well entrenched and expanding. And the citizen with the average income has over forty percent of his income taken by force to prop up this fraud. And you, dear senior lecturer in philosophy, will see again the Prime Minister of a proud nation squirming under questions about the grotesque failings of the Marxist nationalised health system, until the essential rottenness of its structure is understood.

5. The Fraud

It was one thing for Marx to believe that people should not be in competition with each other, that the work system, wages and private property should be abolished, that people should only enjoy the look and presence of objects and not see them as bargaining tools. It was another for people later on, to try to implement his beliefs. And those people were and are, consumed by the same kind of jealousy and greed, that defined Marx.

What he, and his two comrades in deception, Kant and Hegel had in common was that they expunged the individual. The non-appraisal of the individual leads to the darkest ignorance. And conversely, the honest and determined confrontation of the individual leads to the greatest wisdom. Some ploys of obfuscation the socialists use to keep the individual out of sight is to use phrases such as . . . the community feels. . . or, society believes . . or, society thinks it is . These are erroneous phrases. No society has ever felt or ever believed or ever thought. What might be true is that a tiny number of individuals in any community or society may believe the same thing about any given topic. But they would differ widely on many others.

If I use the words society or community from now on, it will only be used to represent that collection of individuals within any geographical, governmental or electoral area. The socialists use those words as if they represented some sanctimonious abstraction, gluing all individuals together in some kind of ethical bond. There is no such bond. Some individuals may choose to involve themselves in charitable works or leisure activities that involve many others. However, this does not place such behaviour over and above personal relationships.

Is the retired lady returning home from working in the charity shop, any less likely to be mugged than if she were returning from a party? Not only is she not less likely, but her attacker may well live close by, and had been observing who might be the easiest target to prey on next. He would not feel the canonising effects of the ethical bond as he ran off with her money.

When socialists enter politics they sometimes do so having just left the legal profession. They have made enough money from playing with the law as a highly lucrative game. Then in their rhetoric they forget their origins. If it wasn't for the fact that some individuals are wont to transgress against, or injure, or defraud others, they would not have made any money. They thrived on the dishonesty and the propensity of some individuals to take unlawful advantage of others. But now; they speak in saintly tones about community and society and forget that the most common legal action brought in Britain, is one man against his neighbour. The fact is that, we, as a life form are not hugely admirable. Not only do we have the capability of preying on all other life forms for our sustenance; but some human beings feel the need to prey on their fellow human beings as well.

The estate agent, or solicitor, or financial investor, all have some amongst them, who are prepared to rob their clients without compunction. The confidence trickster, the builder, the garage mechanic similarly. But there is one wonderful aspect of solace about any of the former individuals. And it is this. If I have been robbed of a small amount of money I can ensure I never do business with any of these individuals again. And if I have been robbed of a larger amount, I can decide whether or not I wish to gain redress through the courts. Not only that, I would naturally refrain from doing business with an individual where litigation was found necessary to correct a former dishonesty. That prospect of the loss of future business, and the desire to preserve a reputation, is by far the most effective force compelling honest dealings between individuals.

Then it is all the more iniquitous when an honest citizen is being defrauded every week and every month and every year and there is absolutely nothing he can do about it. This happens when there is institutionalised fraud. This happens when a nation is in the grip of the socialist ideology. By socialism, I mean, that system of government which allows the forceful intervention of the State to remove money from one man to give to another, for his exclusive use.

What has transpired is that some human beings have developed a ploy or ruse to get what they want through a system of legalised theft. It is a ploy of the same ilk as the hyena who crouches in the long grass, waiting for the lion to bring down the gazelle, and at an opportune moment, moves in and steals his prey. The ploy is so clearly visible to those who understand human nature. I have demonstrated that there is no such thing as altruism. Therefore we must look at the motivation of the socialist politicians who are so determined to maintain, foster, and expand this ideology.

What is a certain fact is that they are motivated by their own self-interest. This is a truth on the same level as the one that attests to the fact that we live on a planet that is revolving in space. So how does the legitimisation of government intervention happen to be in the self-interest of the socialists? There must be some advantage to them in such a policy.

The answer is that they personally hope to gain from such a policy. Generally they are the type of people who in their late teens or early twenties observed the world and were cognisant of the fact that they didn't have all they wanted, and became angry. They became angry with those who had more than themselves. They came to the conclusion; through the operation of negative thought processes, that the only way to get what they wanted was to take it from those who already had. They knew that, operation outside the law would have incurred certain penalties and disadvantages and was therefore discounted. But they came to realise that there were ideologies existent in the world that legitimised the intervention of a third party to take from a first party and give to a second party.

This had somehow come into existence via the perverse meanderings of an ideology that, on the one hand envisaged the disappearance of the State; to the actuality of an all pervasive, all intrusive State involved in grand larceny.

They knew from their own circumstances that they would have automatic membership of the second party; the recipient party. Many people may become angry about their own circumstances, but those who drive socialism direct that anger outwards. They come to see those who have more than themselves

68

as being somehow responsible for their anger and they come to despise them. Those who have more than themselves are now the enemy. Those enlightened human beings who became angry about their circumstances and turned it inward, so that it drove their enthusiasm, their determination, their passion to improve their circumstances are now the ones who are deserving of the socialist's enmity. For socialism is a thoroughly negative ideology. Those who drive that belief system in Britain under the opaque umbrella of New Labour, and all those who wittingly support it at election time, are saying many things.

They are saying – "I don't have power over my own life. I don't feel I'm capable of improving my own life. I am not the master of my own destiny. I do believe someone else owes me a living. I don't think people should be allowed to go on improving their own lives unfettered. I do feel other people have too much and they should be made to give it to me. I am always prepared to place my prospect of improving my life in someone else's hands."

They are in the same kind of mould as Marx, who felt he was a thing, and demonstrated less ability to control his life than some life forms which evolved one hundred and forty million years earlier. The mentality of the socialist is revealed by some of their unguarded comments.

Like the former cabinet member who suggested that the Head of State ought to be moved from her palace and found somewhere more humble. However, this was driven by the discomfort in not being able to house herself, despite her salary. But it is factual that many citizens through discipline and a sense of responsibility were funding loans on their own properties

69

despite earning one quarter of her salary. And those kind of people were not the kind to be held back by the negative thinking that gives rise to the belief in some; that if some people could be impoverished then they would be enriched. Or the comments of another former cabinet minister, and former communist, that it was, "a jolly good thing that a bunch of toffs should be made to wait for houses out in the freezing cold," while waiting to gain admittance to yet another failed socialist project.

Or the former Chancellor who vowed to; "tax the rich until the pips squeaked". This attitude then brought Britain, the once wealthiest nation on earth, to its knees, necessitating him to plead for rescue from the International Monetary Fund. Beliefs which are enmity driven are destructive, not constructive.

After the collapse of the Soviet Union a short interview took place in 1992 with an old Russian farmer in a remote area. He had been asked his view on preceding events and what ought to happen now. His final words to the camera were, "We need a new method whereby individuals can become rich, then the nation becomes rich." This was one of the most profound statements that had been made on any political programme for a long time. Its truth can only be fully appreciated by those who understand human nature. And the socialists ought to be mindful of its opposite; if they pursue the impoverishment of individuals they impoverish the nation.

There is no socialism in nature. We are part of nature. We have to embrace the thinking of Joseph Butler and not the thinking of the prototype Prussian parasite. After all, he failed as a student, he failed in his first job, he failed in his second job, he failed in his third job, he failed as a husband, he failed as a father, but; he succeeded brilliantly in hoodwinking many millions into believing his perverse reasoning that the obliteration of competition was a desirable notion.

When we observe the breathtakingly beautiful creatures from fish to birds to mammals with which we share this planet, we ought to be aware that they would not have evolved if it was not for competition. Only those people who consider themselves to be helpless, fear competition. It is right, and within the natural order that it is incumbent upon all of us to employ effort in order to live. If the situation were otherwise, it would give rise to the most unspeakable stultifying stagnation.

The introduction of the ideology which sanctions legalised theft has been the greatest obstacle to the intellectual evolution of mankind. It has not helped one single citizen in Britain or anywhere throughout the world, apart from the apparatchiks who execute the policy. For happiness, contentment, a sense of fulfilment or achievement, are never externally bestowed on another; they are derived from within.

The other benefit afforded those driving the ideology is that they are in perpetual activity in exorcising their own jealousy and greed. If they are involved in taking money from those they perceive as their enemy, and using it to assist themselves, then they receive a twin pay-off. And that is their motivation for being socialists. That is how they are pursuing their own self-interest.

If anyone thinks that there is one jot of difference in desire between the most ardent capitalist and the most ardent socialist they are very much mistaken. They both conduct their lives entirely in their own self-interest. However, their motivations are different. As the socialist is motivated by unbridled negativity, the capitalist is motivated by unbridled positivity.

In today's Britain different phrases are used to describe some citizens who have less than other citizens. Those can be: the poor, the disadvantaged, the less well off. But if we visualise an eighteen year old citizen either male or female who could be perceived to fit into those categories, we have to ask ourselves, who is responsible? The socialists purport to give the impression that they wish to provide assistance. This supposedly being motivated by the belief that in a nation of sixty million individuals each ought to be as well off as the next.

But under the natural law, there are but two places only for the eighteen year old to look for assistance. The first is to ascertain how much assistance he or she can get from both natural parents. If none; then the attention ought to be directed solely to himself or herself. If the parents could not or would not assist; then the socialists claim to care more about the welfare of this young citizen than the parents themselves. This ought to give all geneticists a field day of head-scratching and investigation. They would have to consider why a socialist, hundreds of miles away who does not know this youth from Adam, or indeed Eve; is so determined to ensure the promulgation of his or her genes, when the youth's parents are not bothered.

But then the geneticists would surely have observed numerous large gatherings of socialists where enormous sums of money were collected to be given to the less well off. But no. This does not happen. There is just one tiny caveat to be entered into the socialists caring aspirations. It has to be done, using other people's money.

The biologist R.L. Trivers has suggested that many of man's psychological characteristics, including envy have been shaped by natural selection for improved ability to cheat, and to avoid being thought of as a cheat. Whatever the precise truth about his beliefs, it is the case, that very few can see the cheating nature of socialism. There are many areas of human life where government has no business being involved. I will say more on the clearly intrusive ones later. But it would be much more propitious for all if we were governed along the lines of the thinking of the Englishman John Locke (1632-1704), than the thinking of someone from much further afield who took up residence in London under most unusual circumstances.

From Locke's A Letter Concerning Toleration; wherein his use of the word 'commonwealth' meant;   any independent community under one government. He says;

"But the business of laws is not to provide for the truth of opinions, but for the safety and security of the commonwealth and of every particular man's goods and person. And so it ought to be. For the truth certainly would do well enough if she were once left to shift for herself.   She seldom has received and, I fear, never will receive much assistance from the power of great men to whom she is but rarely known and more rarely welcome."

The truth can never be known by those whose vision is obscured by enmity. Locke understood the importance of the individual, and held that all men are free and equal in the state of nature and possess natural rights. In a brief few words he has set out some of the legitimate areas of government expenditure in any era. When a citizen lives in security and has his person and goods protected by law, its not only truth that can shift for herself; but citizens would do well enough if they were once left to shift for themselves. And would not some nations in the Middle East and Asia not do well to heed his caution on the real business of laws?

When some States enact laws to support a superstition, and neighbouring ones enact laws to support another superstition, there will always be conflict between them. For no nation ought to be established on the basis of opinion; but on laws derived from the individual's awareness of his natural condition. And the authenticity and simplicity of those, ought to be such, that if they could be verified by one, they could, without objection be verified by all. And from his essay 'Concerning the True Original Extent and Purpose of Civil Government', he wrote:-

To understand political power aright, and derive it from its original, we must consider what estate all men are naturally in, and that is, a state of perfect freedom to order their actions, and dispose of their possessions and persons as they think fit within the bounds of the law of Nature, without asking leave or depending upon the will of any other man.

The great and chief purpose, therefore, of men uniting into commonwealths and putting themselves under government, is the preservation of their property; to which in the state of Nature there are many things wanting.

Firstly there wants an established settled, known law, received and allowed by common consent to be the standard of right and wrong, and the common measure to decide all controversies between them. For though the law of Nature be plain and intelligible to all rational creatures, yet men, being

74

biased by their interest, as well as ignorant for want of study of it, are not apt to allow of it as a law binding to them in the application of it to their particular cases.

Secondly in the state of Nature there wants a known and indifferent judge, with authority to determine all differences according to the established law.

For every one in that state being both judge and executioner of the law of Nature men being partial to themselves, passion and revenge is very apt to carry them too far, and with too much heat in their own cases, as well as negligence and unconcernedness, make them too remiss in other men's.

Hence it comes to pass, that we seldom find any number of men live any time together in this state. The inconveniences that they are therein exposed to by the irregular and uncertain exercise of the power every man has of punishing the transgressions of others, make them take sanctuary under the established laws of government, and therein seek the preservation of their property. And in this we have the original right and rise of both the legislative and executive power as well as of the governments and societies themselves.

For in the state of Nature a man has the power to do whatsoever he thinks fit for the preservation of himself and others within the permission of the law of Nature, by which law, common to them all, he and all the rest of mankind are one community, make up one society distinct from all other creatures and were it not for the corruption and viciousness of degenerate men, there would be no need for any other, no necessity that men should separate from this great and natural community, and associate *into lesser combinations.*

And so whoever has the legislative and supreme power is to employ the force of the community at home only in the execution of such laws, or abroad to prevent or redress foreign injuries and secure the community from inroads and invasion. And all this is to be directed to no other purpose but the peace, safety and public good of the people.

The rules that they make for other men's actions must, as well as their own and other men's actions, be comfortable to the law of Nature.

It is a power that hath no other purpose but preservation, and therefore can never have a right to destroy, enslave, or designedly to impoverish the subjects.

The legislative cannot transfer the power of making laws to any other hands, for it being but a delegated power from the people, they who have it cannot pass it over to others.

They are to govern by promulgated established laws, not to be varied in particular cases, but to have one rule for rich and poor for the favourite at Court and the countryman at plough.

Locke was an observer of life and of his fellows, and rightly asserted that all our reason and knowledge is derived from our experience. And when we observe the Britain of today, with its numerous rules and regulations and laws we can see the extent of the deviation from the natural state of man in his 'perfect freedom'.

Political power therefore he saw as having its authentic origin in the natural desire of each individual to preserve their property. And so in their own self-interest individuals unite in commonwealths and place themselves under government to provide themselves with a guarantee not originally prevailing. And as was the case prior to Locke, during his time, and now, disputes and controversies arise between men because some are prone to pursue their self-interest at the expense of other men. Hence the need for law to minimise such infringements and mediate in those that do arise. And even when the law is plain and intelligible to all rational people, there are some who proceed with the belief that it ought not to apply to them, while applying to all others. And since an aggrieved party cannot decide their own justice, because of the presence of passion and revenge, this must fall to an independent judge. This judge, and all the necessary contingent apparatus of law is brought into being of necessity, in every society, to protect the many from the transgressions of the few. This arises since every individual has the right to take whatever action he thinks fit to preserve himself and his property within the law of nature.

But more importantly, this naturally derived law would be such as would be consonant with the wishes and needs of all individuals in any society of peoples wherever in the world they may be. And why, he asks would individuals want any other law if they were not corrupt, vicious and degenerate? Why indeed! But we know the reason. Because they wish to have laws enacted, that will afford themselves advantages at the expense of others. This has no place in natural law, but is simply a ruse by the degenerate to have their needs met by taking from others.

Just three years after Locke's death the Act of Union was

signed between England and Scotland. This came about on the realisation that it would be in the best interest of both nations to face the future together, rather than alone; and bring with it a lessening of any justification for hostilities, which had occurred all too often, between the two nations. There has been a common currency, language, and; barring minor exceptions, a common law between the two nations ever since. In 1707 travel between the two nations would have been via a pot-holed dirt track; and from the south of England would have taken many days running into weeks. Communications via numerous staging posts would have been a little faster. And isn't it ironic therefore that today, when travel by road or rail takes a matter of hours, by air a matter of minutes, and instantaneous communications, that many want to break away and leave the United Kingdom. This notion has been set in train by the recent socialist intervention. What possible motivation can there be for this? All citizens, whether they be of England, Scotland or Columbia want the same things in life. They want to live in security and enjoy the protection of their lives and property under law; and proceed with the pursuit of their needs and desires without let or hindrance.

Then what was lacking in the lives of so many Scottish individuals that gave rise to the present day push for independence? No matter how hard one looks it is not possible to identify anything that was lacking. But it is easy to see that which was present. It has been said earlier and will be again; happiness, contentment, a sense of fulfilment or achievement are never externally bestowed on anyone; they are derived from within. But Scotland has been in the grip of the socialist ideology for decades. And because it is a thoroughly negative ideology it has afforded no Scottish citizen, happiness, contentment of a sense of achievement. On the contrary, the ideology fosters discontent. It is an ideology which disperses its politicians into the constituencies where they unashamedly and preposterously tell the electorate that it is always someone else's responsibility to resolve their problems. And the voters wait; and they wait; and they don't feel any more content, or any happier, and there is only one last throw of the dice available. They now turn to change the location of the administration of government. And if they think they are going to be happier or more content when that day arrives, they are in for a rude awakening.

Socialism was the last thing Scotland needed. It has depressed desire, depressed innovation, depressed ingenuity, and depressed invention in what had previously been one of the most inventive nations on earth. One wonders how the Scot David Hume the greatest thinker in the history of philosophy, would feel if he were to know what has happened to his country. Would he be happy to know that most of its politicians were elected because of their generosity with taxes, which were collected elsewhere?

It is all too easy for a socialist politician to go around and say to his prospective voter, "I will give you free housing, free education, free health care, and free food." It would take a citizen of great enlightenment and strong character to say; "No thank you. I'd rather stand on my own two feet." One of the more accurate utterances of Plato was as follows:

"Unless philosophers become kings of states or else those who are now called kings become real or adequate philosophers; there can be no respite from evil either for states or, I believe, for the human race."

If such a philosopher had ever ruled Britain he would surely have written into a constitution the inescapable impeachment of any politician who promised to steal money from one citizen to give to another in return for his vote. Since discipline is much more difficult than indiscipline there will always tend to be in any population a majority who will be intent to take other people's money. It is a curious paradox that the law allows politicians to use other people's money in their bribes, but will not allow them to use their own.

However, there is one chink of light available to those who live under this system; and that is, that taxes must continue to rise. They must rise, because socialism creates dependants, and as the number of dependants rise, so must taxes. Then that portion of the electorate who thought they were voting to get; are now giving, and they don't like it, so they vote for the alternative.

Locke also contended that the rules made by government must be comfortable to the law of nature. But let us visualise a citizen looking out of his window at the entire daily activity of three blackbirds. One sits on a branch all day long chirping merrily, while the other two are busily engaged gathering moss and daub and twigs to build their nests. As darkness falls; is he going to be irresistibly compelled to go out and start pulling twigs and moss from the partly built nests; to start building a nest for the blackbird who has not bothered? Most reasonable people would agree that he would not. But he may well be compelled to vote for a system that allows himself to benefit from the metaphorical moss, and twigs collected by others in human life.

He also stated that the power of government ought never to be used to designedly impoverish its citizens. But he probably never envisaged a situation arising where a government could choose to impoverish some citizens and use the money raised to give to others in return for their votes. Nor could he have foreseen the day when a British socialist government is prepared to hand over control of its currency to others, who are far removed from the democratic power of the citizen. However, it has to be clear to anyone who understands human nature on any level, that individual human beings do not consciously give away their power. For any person to do so they would be lessening the chances of their own survival. An action, given the nature of the life force, is impossible to undertake. However, persons can often exchange their power for some expected benefit, advantage, or gain. Consideration would have been given to the exchange, and for it to arise, it would have to have been in the person's self-interest.

Hence to exchange power over one's currency the politicians concerned would have to believe there was some benefit, advantage or gain in the transaction. And the great difference between the individual and the politicians is that they have no power in attempting to ensure their perceived benefit could ever be delivered. The individuals to whom they have given control are far removed from their personal lives, and it would not be in **their** self-interest to see that those who had handed over their currency were duly satisfied with their expected benefit.

While the individual can quickly recover their power if the exchange to another has not been beneficial; the mechanics of reversal to the former currency would be so fraught with difficulty that the possibility of no gain arising, would have to be entirely absent before any such move was undertaken. The evidence the politicians would need to have, is that nationals from other European countries had an equal regard for Britons as they do their own nationals. What they would need to see is clear evidence of well established people's convergence, prior to agreeing currency convergence. For those in charge of the currency will manage it how they think fit in the interests of their own nationals, regardless of how much difficulty it causes to persons of other nations.

If we can imagine a British police force rushing in with batons, assaulting and arresting many hundreds of Belgian citizens sitting peaceably outside bars and cafes in Birmingham and locking them in cages; then we could see some kind of convergence. If we can imagine Britons breaking the law repeatedly and with impunity, to protect their own economy, as do the French, then we could see some kind of convergence. If we can imagine Britons blocking their roads and ports and causing great financial hardship to those trying to conduct their legitimate businesses from other nations, then we could see some kind of convergence. But what is afoot of course is not so much a federal Europe, but a socialist Europe. We can see this clearly in the European Union's recent treatment of Austria.

An Austrian politician used some phrases that many considered could be associated with a Fascist party. The European Union imposed sanctions on Austria. But Communists are regularly elected to the legislature of both Italy and France and there has been no suggestion of sanctions being imposed on those countries. However, Hitler and Himler were responsible for the deaths of about five million of their nationals; whilst Lenin and Stalin were responsible for the deaths of about thirty million of their nationals. Now unless those in the European Union regard the lives of those killed by Hitler and Himler as at least ten times more valuable than the lives of those killed by Lenin and Stalin;

then they have some explaining to do. But then supporting an ideology of dilute communism themselves, they must regard communism as soft and cuddly, while they see fascism as fearsome and evil. But then as I will show later, socialism and hypocrisy are constant companions. However, both Himler and Hitler committed suicide indicating some acknowledgement of their own wrong-doing, but Lenin and Stalin had no such feeling of guilt or remorse.

Locke also stipulated that a government ought not to have laws that discriminated between the favourite in the socialist heartland, and the countryman at plough. But yet today in Britain the countrymen, who are living in their own houses; and by definition net contributors to the social security budget; have to face laws brought in by politicians, sent back to parliament by those who are net recipients from the social security budget; which prevent them from dealing with pests, that kill their fowl and lambs, as they think fit. This is a law that panders to the sensibilities of those who have never got their hands soiled; and against those who continually have to; to make a living. But when interference by a third party between two citizens has been countenanced for many decades, eventually that interference knows no bounds.

6. On Morality

Enlightenment has been set back considerably in the world because of the input of the three dishonest detractors. They detracted from truth in a cynical self-serving manner and elevated themselves on the back of man's widespread imperspicacity. Their writings have caused more violent deaths than in the entire previous history of homo sapiens on earth. They saw no reason to empathise with anyone. They felt unable to behave honestly, and therefore in pursuance of their own self-interest had to behave dishonestly. Unless we can get to know something of their early family circumstances we cannot understand for certain why this happened.

What is certain is that Kant and Hegel were well aware that they were not presenting to the world one jot of knowledge, wisdom, truth, or enlightenment. They had concocted some ideas in their heads which had no bearing on reality, human nature or experience. And their students would have sat in awe listening to those 'great' men who had such intellectual power to be able to conceive of things; of which they could not possibly conceive. This must have given them a great sense of power. The power to deceive.

To seek to disseminate and gain from that which they knew to be worthless, was indeed immoral behaviour. But not much different from; the advertiser in local newspapers who promises great advantage to people if they will only send him a small initial fee. And when all the fees are collected, the address to which they are sent is quickly vacated. But when we talk about morality we must define clearly and unambiguously what it is. If not; statements on the subject are incomplete. A great deal has been written on the subjects of morality and ethics, but this has been very largely descriptive and not an analysis of that which prevents most of us from doing wrong. And unless those discussing the topic deal with why there can be; the relentless benefactor and the unfeeling psychopath, then they are merely describing and not analysing.

They have asked the questions; what is the still small voice inside us? What is this conscience we live by? Is there any universal 'should' or 'ought' in the world? And if there is not, how can we say that Gandhi was any better than Ghengis Khan? Or how one nation's ruler who is committed to the good of all his people, is any better than another, who receiving large sums in foreign aid puts it into Swiss bank accounts for himself; while his people live in the most dire circumstances? Is there any objective morality that has claims on all persons?

They look to Mill who regarded conscience as the proper authority. According to him we know what is right by consulting our conscience. And that right acquires the quality of being right since it has been prescribed by our conscience. He came to an accepted agreement on the content of morality: such things as justice, love, liberty and truthfulness were seen to be good. While injustice, oppression, deceit and violence were seen to be bad. Agreement on this, they saw, transcended creed and national boundaries. The convergence of the actual content of moral codes meant, for some, that there had to be an objective morality.

In Bernard Mayo's; 'The Philosophy of Right and Wrong', he raises the problem of objectivity. And enquires, if moral judgements are objective or subjective; that is, if they remain essentially true or false, independently of the one making the judgement. He asks if there is a real basis for moral judgements or are they simply a matter of feelings or attitudes? If morality, as he first considered, is a field of practical activity how can it pose theoretical problems for the moral philosopher?

But then he acknowledges that morality is not just about behaving; but a way of thinking that determines the behaviour. This changes the question, why should we do what is right, into, why do we think we should do, what we think is right? He saw that there had to be a real connection between what we think and what we do. But then he maintains that there can be no necessary or logical connection between thought and action because we don't always do what we think is right. Unfortunately this last remark is open to interpretation. But I trust the correct interpretation is that he wished to emphasise the do. Meaning: that he may consider some things right but take no action, such as going to someone's assistance. But everything that he did do; he thought it was right, and therefore felt that the connection between the right thinking, and right act, was more than coincidental.

Then he proceeds to dissect morality, and investigate it in different spheres in the expectation that something would reveal itself that was not possible before. And from the viewpoint of Naturalism he looks at the thinking of those who simply contend that everyone has obvious knowledge that inflicting pain on others is wrong, and helping the sick is right. And because it is a naturalist theory its properties are open to detection by the natural sciences. So they reduce the good or the right to checkable areas which are, the pleasure of the agent, the pleasure of the recipient, the pleasure of most people or the survival of the species. But the willing, approving or sanctioning of the moral good had to be done subjectively so there needed to be an explanation as to how this could have arisen from objective knowledge. So when the naturalists reduced the original moral judgement by offering substitute statements, they were talking about something other than morality. And even if they were able to state a fact in this 'lower tier' it would not imply any judgement of value.

Next he looked at morality from the Intuitionists standpoint. This by its very nature is non-reductionist, and holds that all views on morality are intuitively acquired. But this was found wanting because of the implication that there were things out there like goodness and rightness waiting to be received by a receptive mind. Secondly it left no room for, grounds for belief. It also left out the area of the outward dimension of morality, when judgement of others is as Mayo implies, necessary.

He next looked at Relativism. This denies the existence of an autonomous reality which binds a continuing moral outlook. But it leaves room for actual practices and reactions which are always relative to the perceived circumstances. He felt that the relativists were free to say that their reactions were just some aspects about man in his social state, but they had to explain the derivation of their relativised values. Whether they were, conventions, emotional attitudes, conditioned responses, or whatever. An argument against it, is that it precludes moral progress or decline, and that moral effort becomes meaningless. And within this discussion he goes to some length to describe the

87

difference between standards and principles. Saying that when a principle is used as a criterion of judgement it implies an affirmation or negation on reaching a verdict. Whereas a standard allows a judgement anywhere along a continuous scale. And if the moral standard is fundamental the important factor is; whether someone is good or bad, as opposed to a single act being right or wrong.

Then Mayo alluded to an instance of relativism which Bertrand Russell had spoken of, and which had been responded to by H.J. Eysenck. Russell's view on morality was that there were no absolute values. He found that position to be irrefutable, yet also incredible. He had to go along with the arguments which were against there being absolute ethical values. And yet he could not believe that a dislike of wanton cruelty was merely a matter of taste, such as a dislike of certain types of music. He acknowledged that he did not know the solution.

Eysenck responded by saying that Russell's feeling in the matter had a purely psychological basis. He pointed to Russian research which had shown conclusively that social and political beliefs and values could be conditioned in the same way as Pavlov's dogs. And he considered that Russell had a strong and extended process of conditioning which gave rise to his feeling about cruelty. He coupled this with the view that Russell was a tender minded person, and as such had a nervous system which was particularly liable to form stable conditional responses. Before leaving relativism Mayo concluded that on a relativist view moral progress had to be either logically necessary or impossible. And since it could not be defended on either count it was found wanting.

Next he turned to Prescriptivism to see if that would provide any answers to the questions he posed earlier. This theory holds that the origin of morality is to be found in the nature of man as a unique creature. So all those factors which were aspects of different moral codes, but were not common to all would have to be omitted. This would leave a remaining highest common factor. And those prescriptives which remained, led to the natural law theory; which was to be the guide to conduct by people who were able to reflect sufficiently on their own nature and condition.

For example, two of the prescriptives which Plato specified were, respect for others, and a sense of justice; and went on to say that if someone was incapable of acquiring those, then they shall be put to death. And those writing more recently have stated that society could not survive unless human beings accepted certain constraints on their behaviour. Even though most of those constraints were accommodated under conventional law, they added that since some individuals had limited understanding, and lacked the necessary will power, informal sanctions in the form of moral disapproval had to be used to apply further constraint. Mayo found that the natural law theory explained why laws and rules existed but it did not justify them from an individualitic point of view. As someone who chooses to live outside the laws, could prosper more readily than those within.

He then looked at the part played by Emotivism in morality. He cited the view of A.J. Ayer who maintained that ethical words were used merely to express emotion on the part of the speaker and to stimulate similar on the hearer with a view to prompting him toward a particular course of action. But he was insistent to point out that these were never statements of truth or falsehood. Anyone who was to describe an action as wicked or abhorrent must feel strongly about it, and Mayo felt this was an important feature of morality. But since emotional utterances are often made without any moral content, this aspect of the moral utterance had to be of secondary importance. He felt that matters of feeling and taste were of central importance and left no room for reason. And if reason was not guiding moral actions it seemed fair to ask what was.

His main difficulty with this was that a feeling implied no reference to future or past occasions and would allow no consistency. He also felt that even if one person was emotionally moved by something it would not mean that anyone else should be, or would be.

He then looked at morality and how it applied to self-interest. He put forward the idea of calculated self-interest or rational egoism as an alternative to morality. So the calculation was that behaving morally provided the greatest possible happiness. The rewards of behaving morally come in two forms; the external identity thesis and the internal identity thesis. The latter of those being the more important, while externals, such as praise, and avoidance of censure were just seen as a bonus.

Plato had seen morality as long-term enlightened self-interest. Other writers on the subject including the Kaliningrad dishonest detractor saw that morality was sharply contrasted with self-interest. And Mayo cited a quotation from J. Mackie in which he was some way towards arriving at the truth. Naturally I shall return to all of this. Mayo saw that as morality was in conflict with self-interest sacrifices had to be made to remain moral, but the making of those sacrifices was in the ultimate self-interest of the moral person. He points out that the unrestrained egoist can lose respect, including self-respect, reciprocated affection, companionship and trust. And the person who does not want those things ought to want them, for if anyone does not then they must fall short of being fully human.

Then he looked at the sporadic egoist, and reiterated the tale of the bank clerk who could embezzle one hundred thousand dollars and remain immune from detection. But he pointed out that this would entail his losing self-respect. And the one act of immorality would change his character for the worse.

It can be regarded as a fairly reliable rule of thumb that the more isms any person invokes on any topic, the further truth recedes into the distance. If I use the analogy of, the pursuance of truth, with the simple act of getting into a car and starting the engine and travelling some distance, it will help to clarify my helpless feeling as I observe people's attempts in the area of morality and ethics.

They open the door and get in, and put the key in the ignition, and turn the key. Nothing happens. They try again; nothing happens. Then they begin to describe the interior. They talk about the doors, the seats, the safety features. They get out and describe the size and the shape. They talk about colours, lights, aerodynamics. They talk about the sales and distribution networks, and then they compare the comments of many others, who have also got into the car, and gone through the same scenario.

But what was a fundamental necessity, was to get out and lift the bonnet. This is analogous to a concentration on the individual. And a recognition that a battery had to be connected is analogous to the crucial and vital role of empathy in our lives. For it is empathy that dictates moral or ethical behaviour. And it is an inability to empathise that allows immoral or unethical behaviour. The extent of any individual's empathic domain is a factor of their psychological profile. The extent of the empathic domain is determined by all of the individual's experiences up to their early teenage years. But the greatest influence over that extent, is the quality of interaction with others in their earliest years.

If any person in the history of human thought has given us truth, from a tiny fraction of their entire recorded utterances then we must regard those, as great people. In philosophy there have not been that many. Not only were there those who set out to deceive, but others like Descartes Spinoza and Bradley who were steeped in superstition. The truth is not something that can be brought to finality, suitably bound and taken under heavy security to a truth summit in Amsterdam. It is a growing body of data of that which we can observe to be true.

And by the above definition one person who can be regarded as great is Sigmund Freud. He was first to recognise the importance of the relationship between the young child and both its parents. Whether we are moved by phrases such as, the dynamic unconscious, psychological determinism or id functions; it does not matter. What he did draw attention to and attempt an analysis of, was the dynamic existing in the interactions between parents and young children.

And what is important to this discussion is that there are practically no homosexual men in Britain who were raised by both loving parents continually from birth to six years. If this says nothing to us, then we are not interested in the truth.

What those men missed as boys was the opportunity to empathise or identify with their fathers, and for their fathers to empathise with them. This would have arisen because the father was either distant, abusive, brutal or absent. And the retaliation against this loss of opportunity to empathise manifests itself in the adult wishing to empathise with father substitutes for the rest of his life.

This point is merely mentioned to emphasise the importance of childhood relationships. If anyone wanted proof; the proof is in the manifestation of homosexuality. Some people think it is a choice; but let those who think this, visualise changing from heterosexuality to homosexuality tomorrow. But more pertinent to this current topic is the morality of the unfeeling psychopath to change into a kind benefactor. Similarly there is not one psychopath in Britain who was not brutalised horrifically in childhood.

The brutalised boy is now grown up. He is twenty four. He has recently been released from prison after serving four years for a near fatal assault. He is standing at the bar in an uncrowded tavern. Nearby there is a group of four men sitting at a table. Laughter breaks out amongst the men, and he thinks they have made an insulting remark about him. An argument ensues. He picks up a chair and smashes it over the head of one of the men.. Over the next two minutes through the use of kicks and a leg from the broken chair he has caused such internal organ injuries to two of those men, and head injuries to the other two, that none survive. Soon he is again locked away. At no time did he stop and think, how moral am I? At no time did he consider the wrongness of his actions. He could not empathise with the men's earlier assurances. He could not empathise with their suffering. When he was four he could not convince his father that he had not made a cheeky remark, and was savagely beaten. In the tavern he now retaliates against the loss of empathy he needed, and in effect he is saying; "I will show you what its like for someone not to empathise with you." Not only did he not consider the wrongness of his actions; but he felt it was right and justified. His father taught him that the way to solve any problem was through violence. And it was impossible for him not to learn well. He did not have to go beyond the boundary of his empathic domain to do what he did, and that is why it was so easy for him to do.

A four year old boy cannot rationalise the wrongness of wanton violence. So the empathic domain is defined before the early teenage years. And so it is for all of us. If we could not bludgeon another man over the head with a chair leg, then we were not the victims of merciless violence. If someone is tempted to do wrong in their lives and resist; it is because the doing of the act would take them beyond their empathic boundary. The breaching of the boundary; which sometimes occurs, is where the notion of conscience enters the morality arena.

Another four year old boy has parents who consider the idea of physically punishing their son as totally abhorrent. They talk with him, listen to him and validate him, and whenever he gestures that he wishes to be held, they hold him. One day while running exuberantly to the garden he knocks over and smashes a precious vase. His mother, even though not happy about it, sweeps up the pieces and discards them. She issues no words of anger or censure.

He is still worried about the reaction of his father. Later that evening when his father is told why the vase is no longer there, he lifts up his son, sits him on his lap and tells him, "It was only an object, and objects don't matter. The next one I buy will be placed so high up, nobody will be able to accidentally knock it over." Later he takes him to bed and reads him a story. The young boy has been unconditionally loved. As he grows up he loves himself and others. He succeeds in all his endeavours. He starts a business and because people love doing business with him, it thrives. He regularly donates much of his earnings to organisations dedicated to the care of people. He loves people because he loves himself; he becomes the relentless benefactor.

Those two boys who had grown into men, had a certain morality. That is; a way in which it was possible for them to behave towards others. Every human being has their own morality. There is no transcendent morality, only the morality of individuals. And strangely; Mayo had used the phrase when referring to human behaviour as, 'less then human'. However, no human behaviour has ever been less than human. Whatever any man has been capable of, whether good or bad he had done so, without somehow, escaping from his humanity.

We must confront our own humanity along its entire range if we are to seek the truth. In his appraisal of Naturalism none of his objections centred on the idea, put forward as a factual statement. And that is; that we all know that inflicting pain on people is wrong. Clearly not all people know it is wrong, otherwise it would not happen. On Intuitionism he makes the valid point on our need to judge others. But when we do, we are making a comparison between our own empathic domain and theirs.

On the issue between Russell and Eysenck with regard to the dislike of wanton cruelty. There may be many people, albeit a tiny minority who would not be affected by witnessing wanton cruelty. But I find it hard to believe that Eysenck would be one of them. And so it would have been better if he answered the question about his own reaction, rather than explaining Russell's reaction. Did Eysenck not have a nervous system which was liable to form stable conditioned responses? Or did he have an underaroused nervous system? And is there any evidence to indicate that an introvert thinks differently about cruelty than an extrovert?

Whatever the precise case, both Eysenck and Russell and everyone else will have a reaction to wanton cruelty precisely in accordance with their empathy. If a young person has had a cat, or dog, or pony in their childhood with which they had great affection; they will be upset and revolted by witnessing cruelty to any of those animals at a future time. But should they witness wanton cruelty to a mole-rat or hyena they will not be so upset or revolted because they will not have the same degree of empathy. Eysenck was right to say that Russell was conditioned; he was conditioned by the degree of empathy shown to him by others in his young life. Had he witnessed his parents, or his grandmother from four years of age, being wantonly cruel to animals, then he would have had no concern for others wanton cruelty, should he witness it in later life.

Mayo's look at Prescriptivism ought to have demonstrated to him, that morality can only be appraised on an individualistic basis. But it didn't. He was not able to find any, 'highest common factor' or indeed more appropriately, any lowest common factor.

If a baby is born into the world and no capable adult shows any empathy for its needs; then it will die. So in order for a baby to survive, empathy has to be shown; and that is shown in the form of satisfying its needs. Therefore no individual can reach adulthood without having been shown some degree of empathy.

But if we imagine a child reaching a stage where as soon as he is able to take food from the table when he is hungry, he is given no more care. That is he has been given the minimum amount of care to allow him to survive. From there onwards he suffers emotional and physical cruelty until he is eighteen. Now we have one adult with a certain morality. He will see the world as a hostile, frightening, terrifying place, where people are all potential enemies. His subsequent behaviour may well be regarded as amoral by others, and he may well offend against many people, but he still has some sense of morality because he survived.

From his moral perspective, to the perspective of the young adult who has had unconditional love all his life, there is a morality for every other single individual. And it is because of this fact that some have been persuaded that there is somehow a transcendent morality.

When Mayo looked at Emotivism he ought to have asked the question if reason was so important; why some people used reason to guide their moral actions and others did not? Was the implication, that some people were incapable of using reason? The reason anyone describes an act as wicked or abhorrent is because it offends against that with which they can empathise. If there is no empathy there can be no emotional response. He made the point that moral judgements refer beyond the particular case, in a way in which feelings do not. But did he imagine that feelings were generated on a day to day basis or on an event to event basis? He could not have been an avid observer of human beings if he did not recognise that a person's feelings about any issue will not vary much from decade to decade. In fact all 'oughts' are preceded by feelings. And feelings are the reflection of the empathy domain.

Naturally when he considered morality and self-interest, he could not fail to reveal contradictions. On the one hand it is stated that calculated self-interest is an alternative to morality, and on the other that behaving morally is securing the greatest possible happiness. And one of those who had said that morality was against self-interest was J. Jackie. Mayo uses a quotation from him, in which he states that the reason for things going badly in the natural run of affairs is due to; a series of limitations. Limited resources, information, intelligence, rationality, but most importantly, limited sympathies. And given that sympathy is that state of being; simultaneously affected with a feeling similar or corresponding to that of another sympathy is not possible, without the availability in consciousness of empathy. There can be no sympathy unless one human being is able to use their imagination and place themselves in the position of another. But Mackie would have had to understand human nature in order to be able to go on to see, why sympathy was in shorter supply than he might like. And it was clear that he did not understand human nature when he went on to say that;

"men are more concerned with their selfish ends than with helping one another."

But the phrase 'helping one another' implies reciprocation,

and therefore would be in the self-interest of all. Therefore his word, selfish, intonating denial is inappropriate.

Mayo had made the point that; while it was obvious his reason for wanting other people to be moral, he did not see such obvious reasons for wanting to be moral himself. He felt he was making sacrifices being moral, and perhaps he would be better off if he did not want to be moral. But nobody ever wants to be moral. I feel quite certain that in all human interactions not one person has sat in front of another in conversation and used the phrase; "I want to be moral", in any degree of seriousness. We are, or we are not moral, in the estimation of another. If Mayo or any of those writing on morality had indulged in the most meagre act of introspection; they would not be able to say the things they do.

If I feel I need to take the waiting out of wanting and decide to rob a bank at gun point; what are the thoughts that run through my head? Where can I buy a gun? Should I use some associates or try to go it alone? If I use associates, can I trust them not to turn their weapons on me in the countryside when we are counting out our money? Will I have to shoot somebody? If we have to wait for the time-lock on the safe, will we be rushing out, when the police are rushing in? If I get away with it for six months, and am then caught, how many years would I have to spend in prison? What would my family and friends think about me when I came out of prison? It is worth it? Everything considered; no. Does refraining from doing wrong make me a good man? Most definitely not. I live my life entirely in my self-interest and given my empathic domain it would not be possible for me to rob a bank. This domain was largely determined by my parents showing respect for other people's property, and never stealing anything in their lives. And if Mayo and others think they are making a conscious decision to be moral, they are mistaken.

The two more important ways that he tried to demonstrate that being moral was not in one's self-interest were as follows. Firstly, because the doing of wrong generates feelings of guilt and remorse, it is renounced in order to avoid this unpleasantness. But he suggests; apparently in all seriousness, that a drug could be developed which would act as a conscience-killer or moral tranquilliser and therefore people could take this drug and do what they liked. This does not merit a serious response.

Secondly; the feelings of guilt and remorse, he felt, are not just associated with the wrong act; they are feelings tied to thoughts about the act. Then he said:

"If there are no reasons whatever for something being wrong, then it can't be wrong, and feeling guilty about it can't be the one and only reason for it being wrong."

The first part of this sentence is a complete red herring. If something is not wrong then it has no place in a moral debate. And if it is not wrong no guilty feelings would have been aroused. Or, indeed give any justification for the last word in the sentence to be used. What he could have said with more legitimacy is: There must be more than feeling guilty about something for a concept of wrongness to be in the mind of the doer. There certainly is. And that is the belief; that the act was wrong. And if that belief is held sincerely in the mind of someone about to do wrong, then they just could not bring themselves to do it.

But then offenders will be heard in interviews where, when

asked if they knew what they did was wrong, they will confirm that they did. However, this answer is given because they feel it is what the interviewer wishes to hear. But in the commission of the wrong act they felt justified, and had a belief at the time in the rightness of the act, which overrode their per se utterance that it was wrong.

And where does Mayo feel that the belief in the wrongness of something is derived from? If it is atmospheric pressure then all human beings would behave similarly. Whether in perpetual avoidance, or doing of wrong. He was correct to say that feelings are tied to thoughts, but both of those are the manifestation of the content of the empathic domain. He had tried to show or managed to convince himself that morality was somehow external to self-interest. And he moved on, with the word 'somehow' being the question-begging one.

He then looked at how the egoist or consistently selfish person, would fare in life. Note, this was purely hypothetical! He envisaged this person losing respect, including self-respect, reciprocated affection, companionship and trust. He asserted that a life without these would be unimaginably bleak. It never occurred to him that if he were living somehow differently, then he was doing so, to avoid this bleakness. And the avoidance of this would have been in his self-interest. He felt that if the behaviour of the consistently selfish person could be somehow imagined, the position would be of no interest to him because the circumstances would be so far removed from the conditions of ordinary life that it would not pose a real question.

Then he went to say that if some person was consistently selfish then they ought to want those things like self-respect, companionship, etcetera. And the person who did not care for any of those, must fall short of being fully human. We really do have to remind ourselves here that Mayo was trying to show that behaving morally was at variance with self-interest. Whatever the kind of behaviour that Mayo was envisaging seemed to be such that the person would be excommunicating themselves from the human race. And one wonders how that would be in any person's self-interest, considering our status as social animals.

The above hypothesised individual was envisaged as displaying consistent self-interested behaviour. But then he considered the person who could engage in sporadic or single acts of immoral behaviour. He told the tale of the bank clerk who could embezzle one hundred thousand dollars and get away without suspicion or detection.

The clerk proceeds to do so. I am not one for conjecture; it is much easier to deal with reality head on. But when someone uses an imaginary tale it would be better to adhere to the details of the tale when analysing the outcome. It is stipulated about this clerk, that he never wants to commit a similar act again. That he doesn't have a worrisome disposition and does not dwell on past misdeeds. He is blessed with a happy temperament and does live happily ever after.

Mayo goes on to explain why this immoral act would be contrary to his self-interest. He says that the clerk's moral reputation is lowered in his own eyes. And this will adversely affect him in two ways. One; he gets more respect than he knows he deserves, and this causes a loss of his self-respect. And secondly; because he has committed one bad act he knows he is capable of committing others. This then could lead to other steps on the road to corruption, and a changing of his character for the worse. And the knowledge of this gnaws at him daily and led to the reasoning that this one act was against his self-interest.

Not one aspect of the analysis bore any relation to the depiction of the bank clerk. Why should this one act gnaw at him on a daily basis when he has said that this man does not have a worrisome disposition and also that he does not dwell on past misdeeds? Furthermore he says he is blessed with a happy temperament and does live happily ever after. In fact he appears like the type of person who would be very happy with his own cleverness at pulling off such a heist.

Mayo then concludes that having an appropriate sense of morality is the key to satisfying one's own self-interest. So from Mayo's thinking we have those two statements. One: Behaving entirely in one's self-interest is not moral. Two: But behaving morally is entirely in one's self-interest. Therefore if one is to act entirely in one's self-interest one would have to act morally. But since morality is never a concept in any person's mind as they go about their lives; that, says nothing about morality. And Mayo said nothing about morality.

The fact that a person can lecture at different universities and is capable of looking at a sentence in which there is an inherent glaring contradiction, and does not see it; simply beggars belief. Not only is that difficult to believe, but when one considers the thousands of students who listened to him lecture, and make the twin statements; that behaving entirely in one's self-interest is not moral; and that behaving morally is entirely in one's self-interest and fail to point out to him the clearest contradiction is equally incredible.

Thomas Harris came closer to understanding human nature in his work 'The Book of Choice'; in which he investigated the instances of wrongdoing from the individual's perspective. He saw the motivation for wrong doing, in the compulsion of the individual to ease the burden of their NOT OK status. But he never truly came to explain how this defective personality, or NOT OK status, could be so predominant in one, and virtually unrecognisable in another. Taking his method of investigation from the Transactional Analysis work of Eric Berne he did recognise that this stemmed from early childhood. He felt that this defective status in one person, led to the belief that all others were defective, and that this was the primary problem in our lives. And that this status is the result of a decision made early in life under duress, without due process and without an advocate.

He felt that this flaw in our species whether we want to call it, sin, badness, or evil is apparent in every person. But I have been observing people all my life and I can say that there are many good, indeed beautiful people, whose defective status is not apparent. This is not to say that they are not in some minor way defective; but it is not apparent.

This is of course appraising behaviour with the understanding that every adult human being has the right to pursue their own self-interest as does every other human being. But if psychiatrists or psychologists do not proceed with this understanding, then they will fall into error. And what is of the greatest importance here, is that the governance of no nation should be such; as to place a downward pressure on the number of beautiful people, and an upward pressure on the number of defective people.

Harris outlines his assessment of the manifestation of defective personality interaction as a form of game playing. And this tragic game-playing demonstrates itself on the first occasion when an ulterior move is made toward another person to ease the burden of the NOT OK status. But this wrong act does not arise because the child has made a decision that he is defective. It comes about because the child is trying to fill an empathy void. When a child strikes another in the playground he is trying to fill this void. He is in fact retaliating against his parents. And if they were standing close by and they could hear the verbalisation of the expression of the act of their aggressive son it would be.

"You could not empathise with me, at a time when I had no facility to understand what it was about me, that repelled you from empathising with me."

But the fault did not originate with the child. The fault was with the parents. Who; in their turn did not have sufficient wisdom or self-love to be able to give all that their child required. Hence the empathy void. He is retaliating against the ownership of the void.

People bring children into the world because they want to. They have children because it is in their self-interest to do so. And everything goes relatively well until the baby is around eighteen months old. But when this new human being starts to demonstrate its own uniqueness, its own individuality, its own autonomy; the game is on between parent and child. Now there are two self-interests in competition. And if the parent is defective himself the big powerful adult will win over the small dependant child. If it becomes a battle of wills the child will inevitably suffer empathy loss.

Harris referred too often to either; a valid ethical system, or a system of moral values. The idea of such a system is a nonsense. But what must be disseminated through a civilised government, and through a civilised education system, is the imperative nature of the need for parents to give unconditional love and unconditional empathy to their children; if we are to improve the society of the future. Should such a situation arise, and we did not have a society driven by;

"I was offended against, I shall offend against."

then notions such as morality and ethics would fade into the distance. However, it is certain that this situation could never arise under a socialist ideology. Even though he spoke about systems, Harris did say, that slums and ghettos were not going to disappear in society; until slums and games disappear from people's hearts. Therefore the health of the individual's psychological profile has to be the precursor to the health of society.

The possibility of observing those with healthy profiles is available to all of us. When people get to the top of their profession in any walk of life, or are very successful in their careers they are often interviewed publicly. And one of the most striking characteristics of commonality to all those people is the iterated phrase: 'my parents were wonderful'. This will say nothing to the very persons in the nation to whom it ought to say much. Those who ought to understand that parents don't become wonderful because of government intervention. They don't become wonderful because of the size of the social security cheque they receive. Their parents were wonderful because they gave their children unconditional love. And that is why their children became successful. They were admired by everybody as they moved through the ranks, because they had no empathy void to fill. People could not help liking them, because they loved themselves.

At the other end of the spectrum we can observe many others. We can observe the man with the heavily tattooed forearms. We do not see the dentist, the architect, the broadcaster, the teacher, the stockbroker, the design engineer, the computer programmer, the restaurateur, the actor, the pilot, the travel agent, the hotelier with those on their arms; do we? But why not? Why should having tattoos on one's arms preclude one from certain professions? The fact is that there is no obstacle to a man with tattooed arms joining any profession. But it is also true that such men are not dispersed evenly throughout the professions. Why should a barrister not consider those colourful decorations as equally desirable as another man of the same age from the same town? It cannot surely be a matter of not being able to find the money to afford them. Or indeed not having the courage to be able to endure their insertion. Unfortunately for the young boy, who was; and is now the man, this phenomenon runs deeper than a matter of personal taste.

The parents of this boy through emotional or physical abuse or both, offended against this boy's precious uniqueness, and robbed him of his identity. He was not allowed to develop a sense of who he was. What happened in his home happened without much acknowledgement that he was there. What he felt, or thought, or wanted did not matter. When he reaches fifteen years, never having had a sense of security, he feels totally insecure. The world is experienced as a frightening place. In order to achieve a sense of security he joins together with boys of a similar age. He can only confront the world in the company of their support. There was no value placed on education in his home and he leaves school with worthless qualifications.

His parents got what they wanted through bullying, and their bullying extended to him. As he doesn't have the necessary discipline to retain a job, he moves in and out of a great succession of jobs; before turning to crime. He lost many jobs because of his need to fill his empathy void. He was hostile, aggressive and antagonistic. The very presence of persons with healthy psychological profiles antagonised him. Four days after spending three months in a young offenders institution he and his best friend find their nearest tattooist. In this premises he gets an identity.

"Look – this is me. This is who I am. I am my tattoos."

This however, affords the meagrest of solace. The void remains. More and more serious crime seems to be the only way forward; until he is given a long prison sentence. And when we look around prisons we see a hugely disproportionate number of tattooed men who are locked away. And people think that the police, the courts, and the justice system put them there; but they did not. Their parents put them there. And what do the sociologists see or hear? Nothing. They are oblivious to the world around them. They vote for a system that promotes the use of babies as a battering ram by some grown-ups to get what they want at the expense of others. And once those babies have served their purpose they are emotionally and empathetically abandoned, and too often spend much of their lives locked away in prison.

And what do you, dear senior lecturer in Sociology think has given rise to the escalating crime rate in Britain since the nineteen fifties? If you haven't thought about it, what are you doing in your job? And if you have thought about it, and found no answer, then I suggest you find a job commensurate with your abilities. And while you are waiting to get a job doing something useful, you ought to go around and, clean the graffiti off all the road signs in your area.

But what has caused, and is still causing an increase in the crime rate; is the social policy that permits the individuals total release from having to take any responsibility for their own lives. I will return to the mechanics of this later. But I want to talk about a unique area of human life where a crime is committed, but the authorities do not take action against the offender. And that is the crime of rape. I do not include here the one in ten cases where a woman is attacked by a stranger and against threats of injury or death is violated. Those men guilty of such a crime must face the harshest sentences available. But the instances of rape where the man and woman know each other and if seen in the street would appear no different than any other couple. And after a short time or sometimes longer of knowing this man the woman is raped.

She reports the crime to the police and they thoroughly investigate the details of the case. They note everything that was said by both parties, and the actions taken by both parties before, during, and after the crime. They find out where she first encountered the man, and how long she had known him. As the police are getting toward the end of their report different questions which seem to them inescapably rational are demanding to be asked. And they all begin with; but why didn't you . . . And when

109

the woman has searched to find an answer she has to deal with further questions that start with the same words. She starts to sob; but soon looks up through her tears and screams, why don't you believe me? Silence.

For the sake of our understanding we need to know why she did not scratch and claw and kick and scream and shout and smash every object available to fight off this attack; and thus avoid the indignity of an intimate examination and relentless questioning at the police station. Maybe Aristotle knew something of human nature when he wrote this about anger. (I have purposefully changed the gender):

"Anger may be produced by a variety of causes, but, however that may be, it is the woman who is angry on the right occasions and with the right people and at the right moment and for the right length of time who wins our commendation. The deficiency may be called 'tameness', 'submissiveness', 'meekness', or some such name, and it is blamed by us because we think that a woman who does not get angry when she has reason to be angry, or does not get angry in the right way and at the right time and with the right people, is a dolt. It looks like insensibility or want of proper spirit."

However, there was nothing doltish about this woman's behaviour. It had nothing to do with her degree of intelligence, but everything to do with how her parents treated her as a young girl. When she displayed some anger they felt it proper to beat the anger out of her. She was not allowed to say, No. No; would have brought down the wrath of her father. She had to do as she was told and fit within the strictures of a misguided discipline. And her right; later in life, to assert her authority to do, or not to do

110

whatever she liked with her own body, was taken away.

And now after being manipulated and controlled by a man similar to her father she is the crying victim in a police station. And she will feel as much pain, or perhaps more, than the woman who is pulled from the street at gun point. Because, she blames herself for allowing herself to get into that situation. But there was nothing she could have done, simply because of the stunted anger facility caused by her parents. Instead she turns the anger inwards because her psychological profile has been scripted from the instructions; that she must not express her anger.

The day she realises, that her childhood invalidations ensured that she was a target host for that which she endured, she will be on the way to recovery. She will have to take her life in her hands with an iron grip and utilise her anger to repair the deficiencies in her own profile.

Because nobody is going to be charged with any offence, and nobody is going to be sent to prison, the crime of which she feels she has been the victim is the most immoral in human life. But every human being who has suffered the same kind of childhood experiences as she had, will endure similar non sexual 'rapes' as they go through life.

The middle aged couple who have always been nice to everybody; have made an enquiry about a product advertised in a newspaper. The cost of the product was not mentioned. A salesman has been in their living room for more than two hours telling them about the product. They have told him a number of times they cannot really afford it. But he hasn't listened. It's not his job to listen to statements like that.

Before he leaves they have signed a credit agreement placing them in financial difficulties for years. In essence his morality is not very different from that of the above rapist. Neither one of the couple felt they had the power or the right, to stand up, point to the door and say; 'get out of my house; now.' And when they tell their work colleagues about the incident, they may well respond with the same question; of the policeman to the woman; but why didn't you....?

The organised religions have not offered much to morality in practise. If one regards war as immoral, they have contributed to much immorality. One has to ask if the origin of religion has not been in the willingness of some people to claim other worldly powers so as to manipulate their fellows. And that manipulation was only possible by using their own imaginations to terrorise them with images of heaven and hell. The most generous appraisal we can make is; that those religions had their foundations in an honest attempt to persuade people to behave better towards each other. Sikhism and some aspects of Christianity seem to provide evidence to support this. But it is the temporal aspect of those two creeds which gives rise to the improvement of interaction between persons. And it would be better for the world if there was a very considerable shift of emphasis from the spiritual to the temporal in all organised religions.

In other words, a religion that emphasised the greater good in tolerating your neighbour than loving your God. The great majority of perceived sins of all organised religions are those of offences against the person. And the others seem to be related to insufficient respect for a supernatural being. But it is very difficult to see how a Being responsible for the creation of all of the matter in an infinite universe, should be overly concerned with the extent of mankind's sycophancy.

And when we observe the behaviour of the 'salesmen in the field' of the organised religions, we see that they are not at all so keen to buy the product themselves; even though avidly determined to sell. So we ought to look for some evidence of the impact of religious precepts on mankind's behaviour. And this evidence seems far from overwhelming. We can have one religious leader, whom, while abstaining himself from all sexual activity, feels perfectly capable of instructing hundreds of millions of people as to precisely how they should conduct their sexual activity. And while we can have other nations founded on religious belief; when we look within we see that dishonesty, bribery and corruption are de rigueur.

But when we consider the phenomenon of emigration and immigration we are perhaps afforded the only evidence available. There is practically no Christian emigration into non Christian states in comparison to the emigration of non Christians into Christian states. So it would appear that Christian precepts create societies which are more tolerant and more affluent than non Christian societies, even though they may be often staunchly religious states.

And if we are to learn from evidence, that can't be faked, we ought to ask what it might be in the mentality of the Christian that promotes this circumstance. As the Commandments are either creed enforcing or negative admonitions there must be something else which has created this mentality. And there does not seem to be much left other than the precept;

"Do unto others as you would have others do unto you."

And if this is the factor then it ought to; not just form the foundation, but the entire edifice of the new temporal religion. This precept is entirely consonant with human nature and only requires empathic reciprocative acknowledgement.

Do what you have to do, in your own self-interest, but be mindful in the doing that you do not offend against the self-interest of another. For if you do; you confer on others the reciprocative right to offend against you. And the existence of such a situation would not be in the self-interest of anyone. Some have objected to the precept on the grounds that it is an invitation to the masochist to initiate sadistic behaviour to elicit the desired response. But one has to reply that had the precept been the behavioural rigour of the parents of the masochist, then no such psychological profile would have been scripted. And in view of the rarity of such a pattern of behaviour it seems like a trifling cavil. So it seems fair to say that if this temporal religion were to be adopted and coupled with the raising of children in circumstances of unconditional love; then dogma would be defeated and truth would prosper.

The whole issue of moral or ethical behaviour was introduced to philosophy by Plato and Aristotle. They felt the need to do this because tradition was no longer sustaining the framework of their society. They sought to define some kind of behavioural bulwark which would halt the decline into chaos. But their view of society was from the high-minded stance of the aristocrat and gentleman. And the city-state was under threat because of the inherent flaw in its structure.

That flaw being revealed in their superior attitude towards the expected rigidity of the structured classes. The implications from their utterances were that the individuals in one class were somehow inferior human beings than those in another class. Individuals in one class were not expected to aspire towards moving to another class. The slave; or those from the subservient or military class were not seen as capable of reasoning. And this from Plato who did not use his reasoning to define 'good'.

The view of Hobbes of course is the antidote to this; that when we know ourselves, we are bound to understand that the thoughts and passions of one man are similar to those of another. And any system of government which is imposed; that defies the aspirations of the individual; or ignores the importance of the individual will always fail. However convenient it may be for some people to neatly categorise individuals, there is in reality, just one class in human life. And that is the aspiring class. That is given the understanding that we live under natural law.

Every individual aspires toward; a better quality of life, or easing the burden of satisfying their needs. Even the most affluent individual who has no need of making any effort in life, now has to aspire towards providing himself with a purpose in his life. The individual who starts with nothing aspires towards providing himself with a better quality of life. The opportunities for the latter are greater than for the most affluent individual. But when fraudulent ideologies take hold of a society they discourage aspiration, and encourage the belief that the affluent person is responsible for the fact that others do not have everything they want.

So what we would do well to understand is that there is difference, sometimes great difference between individuals but no superiority. And when the diversity and importance of the individual is appreciated, the minority of citizens who have memorised some details and reproduced them in examination conditions, enabling them to sit behind some sort of desk or another; will no longer be unnecessarily elevated.

Some other writers in assessing the derivation of ultimate moral beliefs have made the point that there is no identifiable field of study as to the justification of political beliefs. They felt this to be the case because political beliefs were too varied to form a coherent undertaking. But the reality is very different. In every democracy individuals vote according to their own self-interest. And that is very often a division of the electorate between those who vote to get more of someone's else's resources; and those who wish to retain as much of their own resources as they can.

And if anyone is asked to justify their beliefs; one can soon discover their state of positivity or negativity. And if there is sufficient negativity the politicians who have provided the vehicle for this negativity can get elected. Hence we get socialist governments. But one great curiosity about the individuals who make up such a government is that their most enthusiastic willingness to give to the poor stops at the national boundary. But poor human beings must elicit the same feelings and generate the same response in the socialist wherever they may be. Why should a socialist from Kirkaldy care more about the poor in Bridlington, Northampton or Southampton as opposed to the poor in Bulawayo, Hanoi or Shanghai?

The combined annual incomes of the twelve individuals

from China, Cambodia, Laos, Nepal, Vietnam, Nigeria, Tanzania, Somalia, Mozambique, Guyana, Cuba and Zimbabwe is still less than one third the annual income of one Briton. But why should concern for the poor stop at the border when a hunger pang must feel the same wherever it is felt in the world? If it is morally right to look after the poor, how come that morality is so finite? But the socialist will speak in precisely the same manner about the national interest as the non-socialist. And they do this because they know that the impoverishment of their nation would adversely affect them, and therefore they would oppose anything which was not in the national interest.

But let us imagine the imposition of a world government for the moment; a socialist world government. It would have to introduce such policies whereby so much money was removed from Britain that the income of every citizen, including the socialists, was reduced by at least fifty percent. But given their repeated utterances about the national interest when the issue of handing over control of Britain's currency to others is mooted, they would certainly have to object to this. But their objection would be entirely hypocritical. And they would object because they now no longer benefit from the votes cast in favour of this socialist world government. They begin to loose personally as a result of some people giving their money to others; whereas currently in Britain they benefit from the taking of other people's money to give to them. So, somewhat perversely, the individual within the socialist state is fair game, but the individual nation within the jurisdiction of the one socialist world government is not fair game.

Before leaving this section on morality it would be right to answer one last question posed by Mayo. He asked, if there are formal institutions where people can study to take up all manner of professions, why is there no teaching on the subject of goodness or virtue? But there can be no teaching of this subject because it is not a matter of assimilating facts or information. But virtuous or non offending behaviour is a matter of how the growing child was made to feel because of the absence or presence of empathy from others. If a child has had both natural parents, or some other variation of care giving involved in their upbringing, then they, will be the architects of their empathy domain; and therefore the architects of their morality.

And in order to explain this a little further, I will set out the concept of the empathic domain of a habitual petty criminal. If we visualise a pie chart with, for example, ten segments with a small circle in the centre describing the nature of the individual. In each of those segments is written a possible target area where an offence could be committed. But three of those areas; minicab drivers, own team football supporters, and old ladies with blue hair, are bounded by a heavy red line.

Those areas are not possible targets, because he is able to empathise with those three. When his mother was unable to look after him, his grandmother who had blue hair took over the role and treated him much better than anyone. Therefore, he is unable to snatch the handbag of such a lady in the street and run away. His brother has been a minicab driver for a number of years, and he is aware of the expenses; such as fuel, mechanical maintenance and insurance costs. Therefore he is unable, having hired one, to jump out at the nearest set of traffic lights to his home, and run off without paying. His empathy toward his own football team supporters is obvious. But all other areas he feels free to offend against without compunction.

7. On Social Policy

Even though psychology is in its infancy as a discipline, practitioners in the field have been sufficiently numerous for it to have thrown up something useful in the area of social policy before now. But, alas, anything useful that has ever been said by the few has been effectively ignored or overshadowed by the utterances of the many. The social policies which purport to bring about an improvement in society, could more accurately be described as anti-social policies.

The closed minds who ordain the teaching structure of psychology ensure there is little progress. They ruthlessly quash rigorous debate and intelligent speculation in favour of the fatuous pretence of scientific 'research'. And this 'research' forces students down a narrow crushing channel where they investigate matters on the fringe of the fringe of human life; the outcome of which any ten year old could have told them at the outset.

So the outcome after years of this is, graduates leaving with scrolls in their hands; but also with anaesthetised brains. They then go out into the world and take up positions where, the thought of thinking for themselves has an inbuilt abortion mechanism. If they got what they wanted by not thinking for themselves, they are now enclosed in an action-reward loop, which means they will now focus more rigorously on those who have contributed practically nothing in their field. The issue of motivation will not be considered because that would necessitate sooner or later even unenlightened psychologists focusing on their own motivation. And if this were to arise, some would acquire knowledge of themselves, which would inevitably lead to knowledge of others. But focusing on ones own motivations requires courage and honesty. And those qualities do not seem to be to the fore even in individuals where one might expect it.

There does seem to be a self-delusional obstruction which can only be explained as a defence mechanism to the slightest, but very transient measure of discomfort. But should individuals who are enlightened in all other ways breach their own defence mechanism, then the greatest knowledge and wisdom lies beyond. And the greatest knowledge is that there is no altruism. But those who suffer the greatest delusion go to the greatest lengths to try to demonstrate that there is.

One such was Mary Midgley in her book 'Beast and Man'. In her discussion on altruism she had concentrated on activities that could be seen to have pay-offs and those that could not. And if they did not have a pay-off she claimed this proved altruism. Among the activities in human life she cites as not having a pay-off are; affection, idle chatter, storytelling, greeting procedures, quarrelling, play, sport, laughter, song, dance and lovemaking. With the exception of quarrelling, all the others, either smooth the process of human interaction, or bring about varying levels of relaxation response. She had derived her list in response to the thinking of Edward Wilson, the social biologist who claimed that it was greater intelligence that gave rise to all forms of social behaviour. She disputed the fact that there should be any necessary reason why intelligence should give rise to the list of activities she referred to.

But whether there was any necessary reason or not, it appears to be, that we are the most intelligent life form on this planet and the fact is we do engage in those activities. And when discussing motivation, there is no point trying to visualise a life form of similar intelligence to ourselves that does not engage in any social behaviour. When quarrelling takes place it does so because one person feels their self-interest has been infringed by another.

But the most interesting activity she mentions which is undertaken for its own sake; is that of lovemaking. Even if she is using this in the old fashioned sense, the object is that this would lead to an act of procreation. Now, she is making the suggestion that there is no pay-off as a result of this act. But when we consider any life form we wish, and see the myriad of schemes, ploys and artifices that are engaged in, in order to earn the right to copulate, the suggestion that there is no pay-off gives rise to a feeling somewhere between pathos and bewilderment.

If she had left her house and gone to her local park and waited for a football match to end; and then spoke to one of the young men involved she may have acquired some wisdom. If she had asked him; why do you play football? She may have heard many answers:-

"I play football because I want to keep fit."

"I have a wonderful laugh with my friends."

"I find I'm more attractive to women after I play football."

"I find I study better after physical exercise, than if I don't bother."

"I know the scouts from the local professional football club come here very often, and I hope they see how good I am, and sign me for their team."

But what she most definitely would not have heard is: "I play football for its own sake."

Continuing with her theme of paying and non-paying activities she proves that non-paying activities exist because people deliberately damage their own health and shorten their lives. They do; but again she ought to have interviewed a heavy smoker.

"Why do you smoke?"

"Well, I started because I wanted to look grown up, and now I'm addicted."

"If I don't have a cigarette, I become nervous and agitated."

"I smoke because everyone in my house smokes, so I might as well join in."

- "But don't you know they're killing you?" "Yeah – but you've got to die of something."

She would have found that cognition of the non-paying consequences played no part in the motivation to smoke. A person smokes because the availability of a tranquilliser every fifteen minutes helps them cope with the realities of life, which would be more difficult to do in their absence. So the motivation for their behaviour is the ability to stay calmer in the present rather than consideration of the long term consequences. So the behaviour she sees as not paying; is paying. And whether it is a social biologist or philosopher or psychologist if they do not ask relevant questions particularly of themselves, then the truth will be conveniently avoided. And if neither one is in possession of the truth there will always be areas of dispute between them.

For example, if a British holiday-maker in Portugal, who is thirty five years of age, and who has never rescued anyone before, sees a boy drowning in a river and jumps in and saves him; then Wilson regards this as being motivated by a 'trading' calculation. This means that the man has made assessment for purposes of his own survival; that there is a greater chance of this boy growing up and saving him at some time in the future. Even though Midgley did not point to the mathematical chances of this ever arising, she disputed his rationale, and replaced it with her own view that it was the strong social bonds or sociability of mankind that make the rescue possible.

She feels that we are far too lazy-minded to make the kind of calculation envisaged by Wilson. Even though they both accept that altruism exists, Wilson makes a case that satisfies himself for the continuation of reciprocal altruism, but he cannot discover why or how such behaviour got started. Midgley feels that at one time a great collection of altruistic genes must have mutated, to such an extent that it was a meta-mutation, giving rise to a powerful alteration in the general programming system. Otherwise such a complex sequence of events involved in the rescue situation could not take place.

She had asked some interesting questions such as can a conscious agent deliberately choose to do things that he thinks will not pay him? And; can a trait survive if it leads its bearer to do things which do not pay him? Both those questions arose because she saw it as an obvious point that people often do seem to do non-paying things. The 'seem' was the operative word in the last sentence; but it soon changed from 'seem' to actuality.

And while none of her examples from human life had any validity, the ones she chose from elsewhere were similarly lacking. She pointed to the one incidence when a virus is attacking another life form; and made the point that the virus moderates its virulence so as not to bring about an end to the life of the host. And concluded, that this was altruistic behaviour. But because the death of the host would not be in the interest of the virus, its behaviour is moderated in; as in all life forms, its own self-interest.

And in dispelling the egoist account of motives she points to a particular kind of deer where the stag's acquisition of a large harem had depended on the power and size of their antlers. But those extra long antlers had supposedly led to their extinction. There was no conclusive evidence that this was an evolutionary blunder; and in all likelihood a hungry human population led to their extinction.

When speculation is taken as fact, in countering another's argument, who has done the same thing, the entire discussion is devalued. And having sang the praises of sociability she was drawn to glance at the phenomenon of the hermetic lifestyle. She acknowledges the dilemma endemic to a social species and says;

"awful though other people may be, most of the activities we really care about must involve them."

The implication being, that the hermit is quite willing to forego the activities the rest of us care about. But she is not willing to forego those activities because as she almost accepts, they are in her interest. Her remark betrays her true self, but like the vast majority; she spends a great deal of time trying to conceal it. But what she did do of considerable value was to emphasise the importance of understanding motivation. And what she suggested was that when we have developed irrefutable concepts we ought to apply them to a distinct subject matter. And I therefore, so as not to disappoint her, having shown that there can be no altruism; am applying this to the socialist ideology, and thereby highlighting its fraudulent nature.

When all the froth is removed, whatever colour that froth may be, the crystallised essence of socialism is that a government has the right to take money from one citizen and give it to another. And unless this is investigated from the standpoint of the individual, no truth can be discovered.

In evolutionary terms, around the beginning of the nineteenth century people had been living in towns and cities for a very brief period indeed. And the idea that if an individual could not, or would not compete for their requirements, then they ought to be given other people's money, had not entered anybody's head. And no wonder; for it is not a rational concept. But just as the idea of a supernatural being had arisen earlier because of man's ability to reflect on his condition; so too this ability to reflect, gave rise to other ideas. Some people looked around in their early lives and saw that some other people were much better off in every way. And they thought they could never get to their level of wealth. And they became so preoccupied with the wealth of others, that the gaining of enough for themselves in the normal competitive process was not considered.

Their thinking was akin to that of a young sapling eyeing the great oak, and thinking, "you ought to be chopped down." The Utopian Socialists were at best; dreamers, who had not left their child state of consciousness behind. They were wholly intimidated by the prospect of competition and had to look at other ways of getting what they wanted, other than, through the competitive process. Some people owned businesses and property, and because the Utopians didn't, they thought it was wrong.

And so they advocated various forms of social ownership so that they could take from others, that which they could not earn competitively. Even though nowhere in sea, or on land is there any evidence of such a facet as common ownership; they were able to believe that nature had provided for the common ownership of property. They felt that a natural harmony could be restored if a government came to power and removed other people's property and gave it to them. If work was done they felt that there ought to be equal compensation irrespective of ability or productivity.

And then; when the failure from Trier produced his Communist writings, the fact that some of his utterances were intertwined with the writings of someone who was believed, by the totally gullible, to be a philosopher, their thinking was

126

suddenly legitimised and scientised. Now; instead of there being one mankind, there was acute class division, where antagonism and exploitation reigned. It was natural for those driving this 'taking ideology' to concentrate on economic factors, since it was economic power they themselves lacked, having shirked the competitive arena.

And they could liberally salivate on hearing phrases about public ownership since they then would own part of something without making any effort. But if they had the ability they would have asked themselves some questions about the words public and ownership. And unless we are referring to an ornamental object, ownership implies stewardship. And, was every individual member of that public going to have an equal role in that stewardship? And if not, who was to decide on those individuals involved in the stewardship? And if some individuals assume control, are they not simply replacing those individuals who had control under private ownership? To say that all those who promoted this ideology had disjointed thinking is too flattering to them.

But whatever kind of thinking could describe their motivation, there were others at a later stage who have been described as brilliant intellectuals who gave socialism their full support. A considerable number of those were members of the Fabian Society. But all this proves is the truth of Thomas Edison's statement when he said;

"there is no expedient to which a man will not resort to avoid the labour of thinking. If we bother with facts at all, it is to bolster up what we already think, and ignore all the others, to fit our preconceived prejudices."

And one member of that Society was, G.B. Shaw, who must have gone though life with some kind of intellectual schizophrenia, having written this about circumstances:

"People are always blaming their circumstances for what they are. I don't believe in circumstances. The people who get on in this world are the people who get up and look for the circumstances they want, and if they can't find them, make them."

How can this be reconciled with rampant socialism? It must be one of the most anti-socialist, anti-dependence statements ever made. But if it wasn't for groups of individuals who were gripped by fear of competition and allowed this fear to become their crippling master, this ideology would not have been heard of. And if we visualise just one individual making his case for assistance from a democratically elected government where no such ideology had been heard of, what should be find? They would have to ask him:

Well, why should we help you?

- Because I need help.

How much do you need?

- Five thousand pounds.

The only way we can give you that money is if we take it from other people.

- Well do that then.

But they are using their money to try to look after themselves.

- But I need the money.

Do you think they will want to give us their money so we can give it to you?

- Yes.

Have you asked your friends and family for any money?

- Yes.

Have they helped?

- No.

So you think total strangers to you, are going to want to help more than those who know you?

- Well; yes.

If we take this money from other people and give it to you, what's to stop numerous other people coming along and asking us for money?

- Nothing.

And do you think we should help them all?

- Yes.

But everybody could come along and say they want money.

- But some people have enough.

And how did they come to have enough?

- They either got it from their parents or earned it.

Did you get any money from your parents?

- No.

But you would like us to take money from other people or their parents and give it to you.

- Yes.

Well, because we are governing under natural law all monies raised by taxation is spent on the common good, and we will not be giving you any money.

- Why not?

Because taking money from other people discourages them; and giving it to others encourages very fast growth in numbers of those making requests. And very soon we could have a culture of dependency where all of those energies would be lost to the state, and the energies of those being taxed would be sapped. And since we don't see that we are in government to oversee the deterioration of the state, we refuse your request.

But let us contrast what is happening with the socialist governing of Britain, and the fictitious non-socialist government above. There is a belief amongst much of the electorate that a socialist cares more about other people's welfare than a person who is not of that persuasion. Then we ought to find that if a socialist politician owns numerous properties, he would use them to assist his favoured constituency – 'the underprivileged'. But we do not find him placing advertisement in local newspapers inviting the homeless and underprivileged to come forward so that he can decide whom to assist. What we do find is that he will try to secure the most stable long term market rent possible.

But he will whole-heartedly support British local authorities housing one third of the British electorate at thirty three percent of the market rent. And the only way this enormous subsidy can be sustained, is by taking money from those who are shouldering full responsibility in the market place for their own housing. His support for his local authorities largesse is in his own self-interest; as is, his remaining within market forces to obtain maximum rent on his own properties. The only legitimate area where local taxation can assist, is to benefit those citizens who can clearly be assessed as being at a disadvantage due to some mental or physical disability. And this assistance would be legally capped at no more than ten percent in any one constituency.

For the socialist belief that money should be taken from some to provide housing for others assists him at every election. It is remarkably easy to hand over other people's money to some individual, in return for their assistance at a future date. That takes no enlightenment, no intelligence, no wisdom, no discipline, no restraint and no interest in the long term well being of the individual or the state.

No individual would ever approach a government and tell them to take other people's money in order to provide him with housing; but the socialists knew that the mooting of such an idea would afford them electoral advantage. Of course individuals who are all too aware of being in competition with everyone else, will opt for escaping that competition if given the opportunity. But the facility to escape the market place can only be provided by illegitimate fraudulent interference. The market is a perfect network of forces. The market is part of the perfection of nature.

But the socialists would say that colourful flowers ought not to be allowed to exploit bees and get them to do their pollination for them. They would say that the venus fly trap ought to be match-sticked open in order to protect the fly. And that birds of paradise ought to be sprayed black so as not to make other birds feel inferior. Every time man has tried to interfere with the natural order he has created an ugly mess. But this interference could never happen if there was a total understanding of motivation.

For it has to be absolutely clear, the motivation of the socialists is their own personal gain. Their aim is to gain control over the lives of citizens. With that control they can deliver their votes. They intervene in every area of human life in order to gain control. The citizen who resists, and takes responsibility for their own needs, is the enemy; and is penalised in order to subsidise those who have taken no such responsibility. They need as many citizens, who will adopt the psychological position of the helpless child, as possible. To be able to take responsibility; meaning to respond with ability, to life's circumstances, requires the citizen to take the psychological position of the powerful adult. And those who have done so, will not be in the same need of the socialists' sop as those who haven't.

The conclusion being, that the kind of citizens the socialists are able to trap are those who are less able or willing to take responsibility. Even under the exceptional circumstances of war damage to properties, the enlightened course of action would have been individual compensation rather than taking control of the citizen through public housing.

When a citizen is given a property in which he has no personal interest; whatever level of responsibility there may have been earlier, this dwindles still further. And children growing up in such circumstances witness no regard for property and demonstrate their empathy void with other people's property later in life. So in the early sixties in Britain the burgeoning crime level was brought about by the children of the generation who were trapped by the socialist ideology intent on taking control of people's lives.

The side effects of socialist's control does not stop sadly with lack of respect for property. Because the citizen is being used as a pawn in a game there is no possible sense of achievement; and self-respect dwindles. As self-respect dwindles, respect for others dwindles. But the socialist politicians are incapable of reflection. And it leads us to a situation in the twenty first century where two of the most senior members of a British Socialist government strut around a south London housing estate, smiling broadly at their expenditure of hundreds of millions of pounds; to rebuild dwellings which had been brought to the necessity of demolition through vandalism. The properties were forty years old.

Numerous other properties in Britain have been rendered uninhabitable through similar vandalism even though, of much more recent construction. But not one citizen in Britain or anywhere else in the world, would, having disciplined themselves for thirty years to buy their own property, then set about vandalising it, rendering it worthless. But that which is gained too easily is esteemed too lightly. One would not need to have any particularly special insight to understand that if any type of behaviour is rewarded, then it will be reinforced. So the socialists are saying;

"You can proceed to vandalise as many properties as you like, we are always prepared to take money from the citizens we despise, to build you more."

There may be some people who are deluded into thinking that the socialists' attitude to housing is well-meaning; but if they ponder on the aspect of the provision of housing, solely on the basis of irresponsible behaviour; surely they would have to change their minds. This is the area of provision of housing to single mothers.

Those are young people from early teenage years to early twenties whom, unable to form stable relationships, find that they can get all that they want, through the use of a baby, via the socialist's most cordial invitation. The type of individuals who accept this invitation are those on whom; even though there has been an education expenditure of tens of thousands of pounds; it has had little impact. Education was of no importance in the homes in which they were raised. And hence they were unable to respond with ability to being an adult in an adult world.

In human terms they are at the opposite end of the spectrum to the courageous entrepreneur who in recognition of his aloneness, takes risks and grows, while the young woman in recognition of her aloneness turns away from the attendant anguish by having a baby. The existentialists would describe such behaviour as acting in bad faith. And in one of Jean Paul Sartre's rare moments of enlightenment he said this:

"One manifestation occurs in the person who lives a role or life style that is a mere stereotype or cliché. Overwhelmed by the responsibility of choosing a meaning and a value for his life, a person may find an escape and a superficial comfort in adopting a ready-made role which provides him with a meaning he does not have to make for himself. Instead of living as a subject who experiences his freedom he treats himself as an object or thing that has a designated function to fulfil."

But this acting in bad faith is welcomed, encouraged and applauded by the British social policy. The young woman who was recently, alone, weak and insecure has now acquired the exalted status of a mother. The attention of housing officials, welfare officers and social workers validates her behaviour.

Now her life has a meaning. She did not have to look very hard for the escape, even though contraception was available, at no cost to herself, she chose not to bother with obstacles to her freedom. She has now been given accommodation and welfare payments, and has a degree of independence none of her former classmates however brilliant their qualifications could possibly afford to achieve. She probably would not understand, but she is being used in a very sophisticated socialist game.

That game began in Britain many decades ago when babies began to be valued in terms of points. Babies were brought into the world for their points value. The qualification for escaping one's natural housing expenses was through the accumulation of points. No civilised human being would have asked for such a formula or the devaluation of human life, but since the socialists provided it, many found it irresistible. The ploy of luring people into dependency was working. This was a masterstroke of socialist engineering. When children are raised by parents who are dependent, they believe that reliance on others is the natural thing to do. Especially when political rhetoric is used repeatedly to give citizens the impression that government's duty is to make people's lives easier. This is not the self deception leading to bad faith of Sartre's thinking, but political deception.

The truth is that every citizen lives in a protectorate; where security is provided from external attack, and personal security is provided through the maintenance of law and order. Under natural law that ought to cost each citizen some of their income. There are also other legitimate areas of taxation but the belief that a government exists to make anybody's life easier or better is an absurdity. Only the individual citizen can make their own life easier or better.

How would a government be capable of making people's lives better? If it wanted to make the lives of half of the electorate better, it would have to take money from the other half to do it. And who qualifies to be in the recipient half? The socialist ideology lures people into accepting the quick fix, and once the first quick fix is accepted they are on the path of the life long expectation of quick fixes.

All the people of London and any visitors to the area can enjoy a stroll around, or the facilities in Holland Park. This is a large expanse of land given by Lord Holland in 1840 for the enjoyment of all. And like all philanthropists, he would have, no doubt, given socialist ideology short shrift. Within this park on one of its many notice boards was advice regarding the feeding of pigeons. It read:

"Feeding is cruel. Food left for pigeons attracts rats and other vermin. Easy food means more pigeons, leading to over crowded and stressful roosting sites, as well as a fat supply of fledglings for mice and rats to attack. Easy food means that nature can't operate, making for a scraggy, disease susceptible population. Pigeons spread disease to other birds and frighten away smaller varieties."

The person who placed this notice would not have thought it had any political significance; but if it is so wrong to interfere in nature in the animal kingdom, why is it so right in human life, when we are social and biological animals ourselves? The truth is the warning could equally apply to human life. Those who have taken the quick fix now firmly believe in instant gratification. The welfare payments will never be enough, and soon the credit agencies will be used. When the children demand to have the same consumer goods as all other children, the instant gratification is extended to them. Many years may pass while the debts to the credit agencies creep higher and higher until one day the only alternative is to seek gratification from loan sharks. Then the temptation to start supplying proscribed substances to others in order to pay back this debt may seem like the only way out.

The young woman who is effectively married to the

exchequer, took the decision to engage in this marriage when her psychological child was dominant. The chances of her ever reaching an adult state are very remote. She is now able to focus on how other people are controlling the quality of her life. If only she was given more money she would be happy; if only horrible men were not so willing to impregnate her and run away she would be happy; if only the teachers would treat her children differently they wouldn't be so badly behaved. The focus will always be outward and she will never grow or become an adult. But the real people who were bad to her were those who offered her a way out of her anguish at the most vulnerable time in her life and a way into dependency for ever. And their purpose was to ensure that the conveyor belt of dependants keeps on functioning; and ever widening. A society with a great proportion of non dependent citizens, would not be good for socialist politics.

I have stressed the importance of the need for children to be raised by parents who provide them with unconditional love. But this can only be provided when the parents are operating from the strength of their psychological adult. And I mention this here; because there is a phase in the raising of every child when the provision of unconditional love is not all that is required. This is the phase when the child has reached such a stage of autonomy that it starts to engage in actions to induce parental response. Then it knows it has power. If at this crucial point the parent ensures that he or she is not going to be manipulated by the child, the child will acquire the sense of security it craves; and the behaviour will stop. The parent must win this brief power battle.

However, if the parent is still a child there will be no recognition of the manipulation and he or she will concede defeat after defeat. If the child is able to manipulate the 'child parent' it will grow up with a gnawing insecurity. It will proceed to confront authority figures in society in order to gain for him or herself the feeling of security which was not available in its early childhood.. But it will be to no avail.

The capitulation of the child parent is characterised as, whether real or notional, the putting of a lollipop in the child's mouth to placate the kicking and screaming. This brings about momentary peace, the child parent has found an answer. The adult parent will have inculcated a discipline in the child in letting it know that actions for the purposes of manipulation will not be countenanced. The 'child parent' has inculcated no such discipline since the battle was a child versus child affair, with the one prepared to cry the loudest winning.

This putting the lollipop in the child's mouth is analogous to the inept and counter-productive socialists' interference in society. As the lollipop is nutritionally non-existent and dentally destructive, the socialist's quick fix is individually and societally destructive. Successive chief constables throughout Britain have warned about the dangers of this aspect of the social policy in particular; but it is in keeping with the socialist agenda to use taxpayer's money on an enquiry into the police that denigrates them; rather than listens to them.

The intelligent function of a nation's social policy would be similar to the function of the adult parent who inculcates a sense of discipline in the child. The social policy ought to inculcate a sense of discipline in the citizen whereby irresponsible behaviour is penalised and responsible behaviour rewarded. But as every British citizen knows the social policy is the absolute reverse of this.

Votes cannot be generated for a childish and dishonest ideology if there is a stress on the importance of responsibility. Can one imagine how a political party would fare at election time if its message was:-

"We expect all you citizens to take full responsibility for your own lives, and we will only take sufficient tax from you to provide you with that which you cannot individually provide for yourselves".?

All those who had accepted the socialist's sop would regard such a party as evil, in daring to take away their cherished lollipop.

Should such a party come to power we could gauge what might happen from the reaction a decade ago, when those who had been subsidised for generations, were asked to hand back one quarter of their lollipop. There was kicking and screaming and a great deal of crying, and the government capitulated. The adult parent who raises the disciplined child could have taught the government a lesson. But bullying was allowed to win. And the silent law abiding majority who made great sacrifices to live in their own properties and paid the relevant charges all their lives, just shook their heads in despair.

And now there exists in Britain many organisations and a growing number of individuals who are concerned with the extent of interpupil bullying in schools. This phenomenon causes misery to numerous pupils. And those concerned probably believe that it starts and ends at the school gates. But bullies are the children of bullies. Bullying starts in the home and is likely to be the behaviour of those who have bullied others in the community to get what they want through the social policy. The vulnerable and defenceless child who is bullied in the home goes to school and feels compelled to retaliate against their loss of empathy.

They will seek out the vulnerable child in the playground, and bully them to try to fill the void that exists in their empathy domain. And the child who is picked on, will be the child who was raised by loving and disciplined parents and will not have the capacity to deal with such aggressive behaviour. Hence it will continue. But not until there is a reversal of social policy will the bullying individuals in society, who gave rise to the bullying in schools, be challenged effectively and given no succour or reinforcement through reward.

***

Every person of voting age will have heard or used the phrase, 'a bad area', many times. But one wonders how many have stopped to think why there should be so many 'bad areas' in Britain. What exactly is it about the areas that make them bad? Is it their topographical nature, or their name or degrees of latitude or longitude? Or is it perhaps something to do with the attitude of some of the people who live there?

But bad is a word to describe everything that adversely affects the self-interest of the individual. And since a degree of latitude, or a name or a topographical nature cannot in themselves adversely affect anyone's self-interest, it has to be the attitude of some of the people who live there.

There has been many accusations in recent years of third world standards in areas of life where there is socialist intervention; but none have remarked on the third world appearance of far too many areas of urban Britain. In walking through those areas one sees squalor, dereliction and neglect. Even though in this part of the northern hemisphere secure accommodation is necessary for survival, many have little or no respect for property. Too often where there are gardens, they are strewn with parts from motor vehicles or broken furniture. Weeds grow up to the windows, and it seems the last time they were disturbed was when the nice man from the cable television company fitted the connection from the street to the house. As obesity levels reach nigh incredible proportions and the health of the nation goes into decline, the social policy which generates the decline remains unquestioned.

In some of the so called 'bad areas' there were successful businesses, but following repeated burglaries the insurance companies refused further cover, and they were forced to move. Now they can be conveniently described as 'deprived areas'. Politicians will make the case for taxpayer's money to be spent on regeneration; while the social policies of the self same politicians were responsible for the degeneration.

***

Recently in many living rooms in Britain eyebrows would have been raised at certain disclosures related to adoption. It had been disclosed that many children had been waiting for adoption for up to ten years. And this despite the numerous couples waiting patiently to adopt children. However, all of us who live in the real world; and understand human nature, would not have been surprised at all at this disclosure.

The primary objective of the social worker is to stay in employment. And the way to ensure that that objective is soundly buttressed is to maintain the largest caseload possible. If the social worker was to start finding suitable parents for any child then their caseload would be diminished. And a shrinking caseload brings about insecurity regarding employment, especially if there is an alternative political party who may deem it wise to reduce public expenditure. So every excuse in the world will be resurrected in order to disqualify prospective adoptive parents.

But those social workers will support an ideology which enthusiastically encourages the most immature, the most irresponsible, the most psychologically damaged single females, to bring babies into the world. There might seem to be something inconsistent about their value judgements on the quality of parenting. But when one considers their primary objective there is nothing inconsistent. For there can be no doubt that some of those very babies will soon swell the numbers in the care homes of Britain. And that means a bigger caseload for social workers.

In times of war people have committed unspeakable crimes against others. But the crimes of prolonged torture by parents or step parents against their own children is a crime of a different order. And the burning of children's bodies with cigarettes and the breaking of numerous bones is a new phenomenon. And it has only come to exist in Britain since children were devalued. The role of the social worker is to make repeated visits to people, whose choice of behaviour has caused them difficulties. And their function is to cushion the person from the consequences of their behaviour. Hence no learning occurs.

The number of social workers employed is indicative of the extent to which socialist ideology tears to pieces the natural fabric of human life. There are probably many politicians who believe that the destroyed young lives in care homes, is a small price to pay on the way to buying political power. Like so many other areas requiring government expenditure it is just another fall-out from the fraudulent ideology. But it does assist them in their goal; since all new areas of expenditure means that their enemies can be taxed more. And one of those new areas of expenditure from the Home Office budget is the tracking down, questioning, sentencing and imprisoning of those guilty of paedophilia.

But like the dispositions and sexual orientations spoken of earlier, there is not one paedophile in Britain who has not been the victim of sexual abuse themselves in their childhood. And this happened very often in care homes. Now that they have grown up they feel compelled to retaliate against the loss of empathy. Nobody empathised with them in their suffering as a child and now there is an empathy void demanding to be filled. In the mind of the paedophile, the new child now takes his former place so that he can re-live the feeling of empathy loss in the trauma of the new child. The enactment so verbalised, as always, in; "nobody empathised with me, and I cannot empathise with you." The expectation that this behaviour could change, is as hopeless as expecting any of us to change our sexual orientation by wearing different colour clothes. And one of the most unfortunate things about the psychological scripting of human beings, is that the greater the childhood damage, the less chance of any possible amelioration later in life; whatever the therapy.

Hence, what this does highlight and emphasise, is the vital necessity of a state having policies which encourage the psychologically stable adults to raise children. And those policies by their very nature would discourage the psychologically damaged and unstable from trying to raise children. But to the great shame of a once enlightened nation, the psychologically stable adults are forced to restrict the numbers of their own children, by virtue of having to hand over their taxes, to facilitate the psychologically damaged to bring as many children into the world as they wish.

This is so contrary to natural law that many would regard it as illogical, until they understand the motivations of the socialist ideology. So every area of government expenditure which is generated whether it is paedophile prosecution, care home staff, or social workers, is grist to the mill of socialism. Because every employer, who goes through the motions of pretending to be interested in other people's problems, will vote for the party that intends to maintain and extend expenditure in public services.

They will cast their vote to make more secure the depositing of tax payer's money into their bank accounts every month. Some may not even believe in the rectitude of the State being involved in generating dependants; but since there is only self-interest, even the most tiny nuance of advantage to them personally, will dictate their vote.

And when we consider one third of the British electorate in public housing, and the numbers employed in the machinery of generating dependants, or dealing with the consequences of dependency; then we have to consider the existence of democracy. If so many people are clearly the beneficiaries of other people's money, then quite obviously they will vote to maintain that benefit. But where does it leave the concept of justice when millions of people who compete in the market place to pay for their own housing are forced by law to subsidise millions who are shielded from the market place; even though there is no difference in income between the two groups?

The effect is that the disposable income of one group is boosted to enable them to buy many products; including many health damaging products. When a new derivative of cocaine became available in Britain it found ready markets in the public housing estates. But no politician chose to remark on the paradoxical phenomenon of the underprivileged being able to afford such an expensive product. For having engineered a contamination of democracy, they would not want to draw attention to the means by which they have acquired the bloc vote from those areas; regardless of the social consequences of their policy. Their motivation is the same as the motivation of the credit card companies. Just as the credit company hopes the debtor never clears the debt; the socialists hope their dependants never become independent. The former gets more and more interest; the latter gets more and more votes.

***

When the State intrudes to bring about some desirable circumstance we ought to look at the motivation for that intrusion. For what we really mean is the carrying out of some policies which some people believe to be desirable, according to their political beliefs. And if that desirable circumstance did not exist earlier, we would do well to wonder how it is going to be imposed. If we take for example social services expenditure on care homes for the elderly. Because those, and the staff are provided from taxation, the entire policy implies compulsion.

So the government forces us to look after our parents and grandparents. The implication being that socialist politicians care more about our own parents and grandparents than we do ourselves. They will make repeated utterances about a caring society. And they will imply that we ought to be more caring. But how could a government policy ever change any individual's attitude towards other human beings, or members of their own family? If older citizens are not being cared for already by their siblings, how is the forceful removal of their money and the employment of strangers going to ensure care? Care does not result from some chemical formulae involving taxation and strangers. For how could anyone believe in possession of their reasoning faculties, that other people care more for older citizens than their own children.

However, if this area of government intrusion is deemed necessary then it implies that some people are not prepared to provide as good care for their parents as strangers can. And the effect of the policy is to take money from people who are caring for their parents, to provide facilities for the care of others, even though their own children don't care. Thus the policy is to place an extra responsibility on those who are already caring, so as to exonerate those who are not caring. And this is the logic of how a socialist policy engenders a caring society.

But as everyone know who understands motivation, those who electorally support such a policy do so in the knowledge, that they are going to be the beneficiaries of the policy. They are only too willing to use the leverage of a social policy to provide themselves with an advantage. And the formulators of the policy have other advantages. They are able to persuade the unthinking about their wonderful benevolence. They are able to draw more people into the pay of the taxpayer, and all employees wishing to feel secure in their employment, would do well to vote for the party enthusiastically committed to the expansion of public services. It does not matter that generosity, kindness, affection, and filial love are expunged from the equation. If such human characteristics cannot be expressed in monetary terms, then they have no vote gaining power, and are no use to the socialists.

***

There can be little doubt, that the voting tendency of the vast majority is determined by the perceived likelihood of their being either net providers or recipients of taxation. Those people who look around and see that there are more people better off than themselves, will vote for socialism. They know that if there is a policy of taking from those who are perceived to have too much, to give to those who are perceived to have too little then they, are going to benefit. They know that, on balance, they are going to get the benefit of more services than they are paying for.

So individuals who want to get, vote one way, and individuals who have to give, vote another way. So the voting tendencies of those individuals recently arrived in Britain from other nations is well known. They will have left, generally speaking, poorer countries and entered Britain. And when they look around and see that most people are better off, they support the party that promises to redress the balance in their favour. And the only reason the socialists are so friendly to this movement of people, is because they know that they are going to benefit from their votes in the future.

But if there was a requirement of a humanitarian register, of all citizens, who were prepared to offer accommodation in their own homes, for those fleeing persecution, one wonders how many socialists would step forward. But when we know that socialism radiates hypocrisy; probably none. And while accommodation is provided at the expense of other people, they know that the particular 'homes for votes' policy that they are involved in will not mean their being hauled through the courts at a later date. Individuals who leave their own country to improve their lives probably have more drive, more energy, more ambition, and more enthusiasm than many in the host nation. But the system of snaring those people into dependency from day one; is the most counter-productive act; not only for the individual, but for the host nation.

Even if we accept momentarily that there could be a small number of socialists who are not aware of the destructive nature of their ideology, then we would have to conclude that they, at best, lack wisdom. They believe that stepping in and fighting other people's battles is the right thing to do. But we ought to know early in life that it is not such a good idea. It is instructive to recall the scene in the film 'Key Largo', and the interaction therein between Humphrey Bogart and Lauren Bacall. When she was outraged at an injustice to her father she implores Bogart to intervene. "Do something Frank, why don't you do something?" Most people would probably feel that he was obliged to get involved but, he replied;

"I fight my own battles, I don't get involved in other people's battles."

Had he become involved there would have been a nasty mess; but in staying out, the situation that so incensed Bacall, was soon forgotten. His response was an adult response. He was not governed by emotion, but by his intellect and wisdom.

It takes a very enlightened man to understand his own battlefield, let alone understand the battlefield of another. Our own battlefield is our own personal affair. But the socialist's battlefield is one generated by jealousy and greed. And the solutions they so desperately want are the solutions they suppose other people also want. But if an individual leaves their own country for better life it does not mean they are consumed by negativity. They might well be consumed by positivity, as were the Asians who were forced out of Uganda in the early seventies. And we would do well to remember it was enmity that drove them out. Their positivity brought about their success, and their success generated enmity. We must be aware of enmity travelling via a political ideology.

8. The Marxist Health Service

This is more commonly known as the National Health Service. This is one of the many nationalised industries which has failed abysmally. But the socialists balk at accepting this; albeit having accepted the failure of many of the others. It is a system of health care where citizens are forced to pay five star levels of taxation, to be provided with, if they are extremely lucky, one star level of service. And there is an irony in the fact that they are proud of bringing about this situation. A situation where citizens take flights to foreign countries to avail of an efficient service, instead of allowing themselves to be invalidated still further in an endless queue.

Even though in 1948 eight out of ten doctors opposed the idea, one person who was involved in forcing their hand was Barbara Castle. And in writing about this, which she considers a 'British Great', having alluded to alleged abuses of the service even in the earliest stages, she went on to say;

"You paid your income taxes according to your ability to pay, and in return were entitled to receive free at the point of use the best medical care the country could provide."

It seems that in this sentence Castle was on her way towards reiterating Marx's time-honoured phrase, inveigling the incarnation of indolence, but stopped herself. But even while

151

stopping herself, she was able to pack three serious inaccuracies into one sentence. Firstly, a country can never provide medical care to anyone. Some individual citizens however, in the employ of the state machinery may on receipt of other people's taxes, attempt to provide a service of medical care. To some this may seem like an unnecessary distinction, but if we forget that individual citizens are always involved in the provision of goods and services to others, we will fall into error.

Secondly, the service was not free at the point of use, no more than my advance telephone rental charges makes my telephone free for my use. In fact the service was either part paid for in advance and subsidised by other people's taxes, or paid for at vast expense by borrowed American dollars.

Thirdly, income tax is the forced removal of a percentage of an employee's income with no regard to their level of remaining disposable income. Ability, suggests volition, and there is no volition in the payment of income tax.

When a state intervenes and tries to provide a service of any kind, it can only do so with the people's taxes. Therefore, whatever the service being provided, the people are paying for that service. And since there has been no suggestion that the State can force the employees involved to work for a penny less than they are prepared to work for, the service costs the same the day after nationalisation as the day before.

But there would be no motivation for a socialist government's involvement if there was no political advantage to be obtained. And what is that advantage? The advantage is that from now on the permanently spring loaded word 'free' can form part of their brainwashing mantra. Whilst previously health care cost whatever it cost in the market place, now the nice socialists are able to provide it 'free'. But their justification for their interference stemmed from their belief that it was wrong that some people were able to afford to pay for health care, and others were not.

So after nationalisation those who were previously spending their money on other things, or where health was not a priority, now had health care services available at no cost to themselves. So the system was then constructed on the basis of: from each according to their ability, to each according to their needs. And the people who were previously providing for their own health care were now forced by law to provide for the health care of others. And even though today, there are millions who knowingly and deliberately damage their own health; we are somehow supposed to believe that people were different in 1948.

There can be nothing more intimate, more private or more personal than one's own health care. And the belief that a national government has any place in this, is the greatest absurdity. The socialists have enveloped health care in an aura of sanctimoniousness which is nauseating. And this sanctimoniousness starts and ends with the Marxist idea – and is never witnessed when scandal after scandal is brought to light. When any enlightened politician suggests that perhaps sub standard mediocrity is not sensible for all citizens, they face a verbal lynching with the words, two-tier, being the most spiked weapon.

But when a citizen is unwell, the need of that citizen for some individual or individuals to provide him with services to bring about a desired end, is no different from his need for any other service. It is no different than his need for the provision of food, or his need for an energy supply to his house, or his need for a transport service.

And in an adult nation, run by an adult government under natural law, there would be a multi-tier level of health care available to every citizen. Just as there is a multi-tier level of hotel accommodation provision, there ought to be a multi-tier level of health care provision. There are hotels in Britain where citizens can pay one month's average salary for one night's accommodation. And there are others, not many miles away, where citizens can pay two hours average income for one night's accommodation. But there is no rioting in the streets. We do not find an enormous rabble protesting outside the more expensive hotel. We do not find people commenting on the injustice, and the immorality of the discrepancy between the two hotels. The guest in the more expensive hotel is providing employment for more people; but should the same person use their buying power to access health care they are vilified.

Should the socialists go ahead and nationalise the hotels the standards in both would be equalised and soon they would be unacceptable to all guests. The staff would be complacent and disinterested, and where there were formerly customers, there are now nuisances to be treated with contempt. But the hotels were not nationalised because the numbers of citizens availing of the service would not allow sufficient electoral leverage to merit the intrusion.

When the government intervenes to try to run any service it generates a trade unionised work force who believe that the purpose of the entire operation is to keep the members of the union in employment. To say that the provision of the service is of secondary importance would be to overstate the level of consideration given. And therefore we ought to look at the phenomenon of workers banding together in a union.

If any business is to function it must offer any potential employee the market rate commensurate with the position offered. If it does not, the position will remain unfilled, and the business will suffer. In any private concern in competition with other private concerns, this would not happen, and the position would soon be filled.

However, when unions take strike action, or hold the threat of strike action over pay negotiations, they interfere with the equilibrium of supply and demand. When individuals group together and, as one unit, use force to gain a higher income, they get that higher income from the pocket of the butcher, the baker, the silicon chip-maker. This is more obviously true and long lasting in the public sector. It is long lasting because there is an endless supply of taxpayer's money; whereas, in the private sector, if such action were to be taken the operation would sooner or later go out of business.

Nobody would suggest that an employee does not have the right to withdraw their labour, but when there is co-ordinated activity to prevent the employer recruiting willing replacements, that prevention amounts to blackmail. The law does not allow one individual to blackmail another, but it does allow a group of unnamed individuals to blackmail all other citizens. So in acting in their own self-interest they gain an advantage at the expense of the self-interest of others.

One has to wonder how the socialist ideology which gives rise to this activity can countenance such behaviour. Given that there are millions of citizens who do not need the protection of trade unions to stay in employment, and cannot retaliate, there is now a newly created inequality. This means that inequality is good, if it is in the interest of socialists.

When the members were engaged in or considering strike actions they were attempting to increase their profits. They would no doubt claim they were trying to increase their income. But having paid all necessary expenses from one month's labour, that which remains from the total income is the profit. And if those employees were working in the nationalised health service, how could they possibly feel comfortable about making a profit out of health care provision? The socialists have a great aversion and disgust for the word, profit. They regard it as a cardinal sin to mention health care and profit in the same sentence. But for many socialists this disgust with the word profit extends to all areas of human life. And their objection, of course, is a psychological objection.

Their revulsion stems from the feeling that other people are getting money and they are not. This arouses in them a feeling of insecurity, because in another's enrichment, they feel consequential impoverishment. Their revulsion for profit is the same as Marx's revulsion for factory owners. Even though there is in fact no impoverishment, they feel that if someone else is getting richer they are getting poorer. This only happens in the mind of a negative individual. As alluded to earlier, they go through life feeling powerless, and on hearing the word profit they know instinctively that it is going to somebody who has the power to make profit, and since they do not believe that to be themselves, they feel angry and upset.

To illustrate this a little further, we can look at the many instances when one individual amongst many friends suddenly wins a large fortune. Relationships instantly change. Those friends who did not win are no poorer, but they feel poorer. And however people might think the bonds of friendship ought to remain the same, they cannot. Even though some people set out gallantly to keep everything as before, it is impossible. The winner's presence amongst his former friends makes them feel insecure. And even though the winner may be a most mature adult the friends one by one will construct some imaginary slight to justify breaking the friendship. So nothing whatever had changed in the interpersonal relationship apart from the feeling of insecurity engendered in the non-winners. And this happened because of the constant reminder that someone else was much better off than themselves. This same uncomfortable feeling is experienced by the socialists on hearing that someone else is making a profit.

But if they were capable of a little reflection they would realise that every advance in civilisation, and everything that has taken the drudgery out of human life, has been driven by the profit motive. Therefore, improvements come about because of the profit motive. And improvements come about in the health status of an individual because of the profit motive. If I do not think it unreasonable that my mechanic should make a profit from repairing my car; why should I think it unreasonable that my doctor should make a profit from improving my health? Does he not have a right to make a living? And if he does; is not making a living, making a profit? And if he does have that right, why should fifty doctors working together in one hospital, offering a range of services not make a profit?

And should fifty doctors remove themselves from the present system and set up business in their own hospital while retaining all their former patients there would be an astonishing improvement for all. The morale of the doctors would instantly improve, knowing they were in charge of their own affairs. The patients who were objects, or nuisances would now become customers having their large contributions to the nationalised system being returned to them. The hospital staff would not need to be in a trade union as nobody who is needed by an employer needs to have any organisation ensuring their protection from dismissal. Therefore those found to be inept or incapable would be dismissed. There would now be a real interest in the well being of patients. Currently under this failed nationalised system the health status of the average Briton is such that there needs to be an average of six visits to a general practitioner each year.

Under the private system the doctors would advise their customers on preventative medicine, life style, and diet; and would no longer over prescribe addictive drugs for decades. The customers would then tell their friends, relatives and colleagues about the new improved health care, and more customers would arrive, leading to improved business and more profit.

It would be in the interest of the executives to ensure that nobody gained employment using falsified credentials. Then we would not have a situation where patients are given gas, leading to their death, instead of oxygen. We would not have a situation where medication is injected into the spine, leading to death, instead of into a vein. We would not have a situation where

158

doctors were unable to diagnose meningitis and send their patients home to die. We would not have a situation where it would take nine months to obtain scan results. We would not have a situation where smear test results would be misread, leading to unnecessary surgery. We would not have a situation where healthy organs were removed instead of defective organs. We would not have a situation where patients exhibiting signs of fatal illness would be informed that the next appointment available would be in three years. We would not have a situation where enormous sums of money were wasted as a result of failing to source more competitively priced materials. We would not have a situation where police investigations were necessary to deal with those swindling money from the system by presenting concocted invoices. Or we would not have a situation where, 'do not resuscitate' notices were attached to the beds of some patients, who were considered a greater nuisance than some others.

But all of those things go on in the nationalised health service. And it would be unfortunate if attention drawn to those ills detracted from the essential rottenness of the system which is corrupt from its core to its extremities. And the most powerful aspect of that corruption is the inherent implication that the health of the individual is someone else's responsibility. This causes enormous problems.

The socialist state is in effect saying to every individual, "your health is our responsibility. We have taken the responsibility away from you, because we believe that is the right thing to do. We will find the money to look after you regardless of what you do." And unfortunately, but not surprisingly, many citizens have relinquished all responsibility for their own health, safe in the knowledge that the cost of the consequences of that neglect will be met by someone else.

The import of the socialist interference creates an infantile attitude in the minds of many citizens. They hold on to the belief; "they will always look after me." But if they understood human motivation they would not be so deluded. Like the child suffering emotional abuse from its parents, those citizens cannot believe that the government would cause them harm. But as the psychologically damaged parent wants power over a little child, the socialists driven by enmity do great harm to a nation in their quest for power. And through this infantilisation of the British people, one person in every eight is now disabled; which was certainly not the case in 1948.

But like the destroyed children in care homes, the ill health of the nation is a small price to pay so as to be able to use the leverage of increased expenditure in the system at election time to buy votes. After all, how could the millions who have been drawn into a condition of ill health be expected to vote for an alternative government, that might place more emphasis on personal responsibility? However, all of those who do rely on the government pushing drugs into their hands, have to ask themselves a very serious question. Why did they ever believe that a government cared more about their health than they did themselves? When a government is simply other people; where is the logic in this belief?

What those people have to understand is that the socialist interference was for the purposes of gaining control over people's lives, and by definition, control over their votes. Over the past thirty years the varied field of alternative medicine has proved itself to be highly effective in alleviating much ill-health. But the nationalised service has not been moved other than to be dismissive. There is a very good reason for this. For a citizen to be interested in homeopathic or herbal medicine, it would imply that they were taking an interest in their own health. It would imply that they had a part to play in staying healthy. But that kind of an attitude must not be encouraged.

If a lot of people started to take an interest in their own health, then the ability to manipulate them at election time would be lost. But unfortunately for the democratic process, many people are easily manipulated. Sometimes the thought processes of individuals assist the intention of the nationalised service. They feel that because they are contributing a great deal in taxation they might as well make use of the system and get value for money. So they seek assistance for minor ailments which would be better left to resolve themselves.

Then there are those people who, because of their life circumstances, never have much sense of their own importance. So if they are able to tell people that they have been prescribed antibiotics they will glean some importance from the interaction. Some bacteria felt the person was important enough to attack, and a state employee in the role of dispensing drugs, felt the person was important enough to be provided with a medication that would obliterate all bacteria good and bad. The general practitioner has come to learn that; this time honoured sop is the quickest way of bringing about an end to any consultation. So if he is happy, and the patient is happy, and the pharmaceutical company is happy; why should anyone see anything wrong in any of this? The ever so slight objection, is that many of the people registered disabled have been brought to their state of ill health by the over prescription of drugs, including antibiotics.

One of the most unfortunate aspects of all of this is that most of those who studied medicine set out with high ideals. They probably expected to have a high degree of job satisfaction. But when they have the same few minutes to spend with the person who does everything to try to remain healthy, as the person who is most determined to damage their own health, the high ideals are soon lowered. High morale and job satisfaction are not possible in a Marxist system. For just as all patients are things, so too, all employees are just things. The high ideals go the same way as the enterprising and industrious in a communist state.

They become submerged by the overwhelming malaise. Why do things become so bad? They become so bad because a socialist system is a negation of self-interest. And if you negate self-interest you eradicate authenticity. If human nature is not understood, the clarity of why socialism has to fail may not be obvious. If you take a successful manager from private enterprise and ask him to manage a nationalised health service, something enormously important changes in his first day in his new job. And this is; his attitude. He is now insulated from the market place.

Now he is not in competition with anyone. He can relax, there is nothing to prove. He has got nothing to do with generating the money to run the service. Taxpayers provide the money. And if the service fails, they will be forced by the socialist government to pay more tax, in the vain attempt to force it to succeed. He is not concerned with profit or loss or success or failure. He is just one among thousands of managers, and nobody has any interest or motivation in comparing one with another. The service he works in, is a monopoly, and the success cannot be gauged against any other service.

The success as far as the socialists are concerned is that the monopoly exists. The function of the monopoly has no other purpose than to manipulate votes. He becomes aware very soon that promotion only arises through seniority. He will have to wait. But he would perhaps settle for feeling more important. So he asks a senior manager for an assistant to help him with his burdensome clerical duties. He gets his assistant. And this person will come in very useful should there have to be any shifting of responsibility. And if a government should ever come to power which was not so sympathetic with Marxist ideology, and consider the service absurdly over bureaucratic, he has a buffer zone between himself and redundancy. All he has to do is make himself look good. He has to be friendly to those below him; diplomatic to those alongside him and sycophantic to those above him. Within months he is the ideal civil servant.

He will have lost his raw, vibrant, energetic enthusiasm, and at his numerous meetings he will be able to speak a lot, and say nothing. When he discovers that many of his colleagues take three weeks per year away from work through illness, he also becomes unwell for more often than when he worked in private industry. After all, who cares – its only taxpayer's money? It's not as if he is going to be confronted in the street by a taxpayer and accused of stealing his money. So if anybody outside the political purpose of this nationalised industry believes that there can be motivation other than that driven by self-interest, they would need to be tragically deluded.

And then when the failure continues, since the thinking behind its inception and continuation is fatally flawed, some citizens have the effrontery to complain about the service. And

163

then when those complaints become a little embarrassing for the apologists of the service, they deflect them by a number of strategies. They set up a 'working party' to discover why its all going wrong. They generate another 'consultative document'. They carry out a 'reappraisal of standards'. They instigate a 'new initiative'. They express enormous optimism in a new 'feasibility study'. And when all this comes to nought; and when thousands of civil servants have banked their pay cheques, alas and alack, their combined intelligence has attributed the cause of the failure to be; 'lack of resources'.

And then we have the spectacle of a British Prime Minister making plaintive cries for more time to put it right. More time to put in more resources. More time to take more taxes from the already abused and deluded population. Already abused by the disgraceful service available, and deluded if they ever think it will ever work regardless of the money spent. Their extra expenditure is akin to a man buying a new piece of timber from a store, and placing it against a large wooden structure already eaten through with woodworm. For the fact is; and this is not conjecture, supposition or prejudice, the fact is, that socialism fails. It fails no matter where it is tried in the world. It has destroyed every country that has experimented with the ideology. And even when people come into Britain hidden in goods containers, or under trains, or clinging to aircraft from failed socialist states, the socialists in Britain will still not accept that the application of socialist ideology is bound to fail. The only reason the Marxist health service can stay in existence is because it is a voracious leech on a largely capitalist economy. If it was not for the success of individuals external to the government machine generating wealth, because of their self-interest, the twin vote buying forces of a welfare state and a Marxist health service could not be sustained.

But one wonders how long it will be; as taxation starts to rise steadily above forty percent, to pay for the increasing number of dependants, and to fund the still failing Marxist health service before they start to question that which they had earlier given their support?

Overwhelming evidence has emerged from nations where there is a genuine interest in health, that what goes on inside one's head has the greatest bearing on one's physical health. And within that stream of thoughts the extent to which one is in control of one's own life is the most crucial factor. And if a political ideology deludes peoples into relinquishing control of their own lives, their health will suffer.

And hence we observe in Scotland the most socialist nation in western Europe that the health of the people is by far the worst in western Europe. There is no surprise in this to anyone who understands human nature. This has come about because there has been the greatest extent of infantilisation in that country than elsewhere. The socialists have patted them on the head and said; "There's no need for you to take any responsibility for any aspect of your life whatsoever; we will do everything for you; all we ask, is that you trot out at each election, and send back a socialist to parliament." - And they duly oblige. But this succumbing to the socialist sop exerts a heavy price. For an individual who is not in charge of their own life is perpetually on a sea of stress. Other people will have control of all of their strings. And they will use those strings in their own self-interest and not in the interest of the dependant.

While every single Scot, just as every single Eskimo will try to do everything in their own self-interest, the advancing of that self-interest is now shackled, since they have handed over control. And the frustration brought about by this situation manifests itself in anxiety disorders, liver disease, lung disease and heart disease.

And why should the Scottish be generally more unhealthy than, for example, the Cubans? There is a very good reason for this, and it is important to understand why. While all Cubans are equally poor, some of them do not have the opportunity of looking around and seeing others in charge of their own lives and making strides towards greater personal freedom. Hence no envy is aroused. But in Scotland many people have abjured the temptation to become locked into dependency, and are in control of their own lives. As each year goes by they become better off and attain the means to allow themselves to enjoy life as they wish. This brings about an ever more acute disparity, causing envy and enmity in those who have become 'locked in'. And while every thought affects the body, enmity in particular impairs health. Many will find that the best way of easing the discomfort is to anaesthetise themselves with some kind of substance, which will lead very soon to their reliance on the Marxist health service.

It is perhaps instructive to illustrate a little further the presence of the enmity factor in people's lives. This may in some degree affect everyone. But it is a matter of degree. In recent times some people have suggested that in television news reporting there ought to be more emphasis on good news. But no action was taken as a result of this suggestion. Those who were in possession of audience figures, in relation to programme content, saw to that. They were well aware that people do not want to look at good news. They switch off good news. And since the purpose of the television company is to retain the largest audience possible, good news has to be omitted. And the reason why people do not want to look at good news is the same as the socialists' revulsion on hearing the word profit. It makes them feel insecure.

As we go through life we are continually exposed to hazard and possible disaster. No meticulous planning can safeguard us against great uncertainty. We face the threat of injury or death from a variety of sources. We have to observe unnecessary suffering, cruelty and injustice. And what we crave for, perhaps too much, is a sense of security. And when people are at rest, in their comfortable homes, in their comfortable armchairs, they do not want to hear about the twenty four year old who started his own business two years ago and is now a multi-millionaire . They are more comfortable observing a natural disaster in Central America where ramshackle homes are being swept away in a frightening torrent. While other people's lives are being ruined, they remain in their strong dwelling, which is in no danger of being swept away, and they feel secure in that knowledge. Whereas, a success story about another human being would remind them of how different they are, and make them feel uncomfortable. So a succession of good news stories would have to be switched off. But a succession of stories about other people's misfortunes would provide the sense of security people crave.

Just as the person driving on the motorway on seeing an accident on the adjacent carriageway slows down to take in the full scene of carnage. This gives him a feeling of security in the knowledge that other people have had a great misfortune and not him. This is not rational behaviour, but the more insecure the individual the more likely he is to engage in this behaviour. For the feeling of security must be obtained wherever it can be found. And the attraction of the feeling has the power to override the danger inherent in this activity. So we can be in no doubt about the manner in which events surrounding some human beings, have the power to impact on another human being's feelings. And it is the insecure person's preoccupation with the circumstances of others that leads to jealousy. And jealousy leads to enmity. And because there are so many people with irrational thought processes, the wind for the socialist sail is produced.

For if we compare our health insurance premiums paid to the State, with our premiums paid for our motor vehicles we find remarkable differences. Not one person would be inspired to comment on the irrationality of how motor vehicle insurance is structured. And that is because it is entirely rational. The more irresponsible you are as a driver the more you pay. This is the essential equilibrium between the insurance company and the insured. The person considering driving recklessly is constrained by consideration of his own bank account. This logical structure leads to a situation where British roads are amongst the safest in the world on which to drive. The insured has a choice of many highly efficient, highly competitive, private companies from which to buy his insurance.

But should we follow through a horrific imaginary chain of events when a socialist government nationalised this service; and observe what happens to a man who has driven carefully for twenty years but is now involved in a serious collision.

When he tries to avail of the service he has paid for over a very long time, he will be met with disinterested staff, unanswered telephone calls, broken appointments and a date many months ahead when the prospect of getting his car repaired might be possible. He doesn't find this very satisfactory and pleads for some way at getting his car repaired a little sooner. He is then told that there is a much shorter waiting period at a garage two hundred miles away. But when he gets there, on the due date, he discovers that there is a new policy in operation of only repairing vehicles with minor damage, in order to reduce the highly criticised waiting lists.

The unionised staff involved in this man's invalidation are guaranteed their wages and salaries next week, and next month, and next year, so why should they be concerned for their customer? However dissatisfied he may be, he is bound by law to continue paying for a service which is thoroughly contemptuous of him as a human being, and contemptuous of the relationship between service provider and customer. Not only would he have to endure this, but his premiums would probably be ten times greater; and he would have to resign himself to paying for the repair bills of the reckless. Of which there would be many, given the absence of connection between behaviour and consequence.

It is necessary to acquire an understanding of the change of behaviour and attitude of those employed under the protection provided by socialist interference. For there can be no doubt that they would behave differently if they were subject to the normal rigours of the market place that existed everywhere, before this ideology gained popularity.

An aircraft accident occurred recently where all passengers and crew died. This happened as a result of fuel tanks being pierced by debris, resulting in fire. There were many civil servants employed with the task of ensuring that this did not happen. They were provided with money from taxpayers to ensure the highest level of safety standards possible. It is a natural aspiration of citizens to feel that high standards are maintained in the manufacture and maintenance of aircraft. But then when we learn that there had been over fifty warnings of the possibility of this fire happening, we can understand something about; attitude.

The department in which they are employed demands the most rigorous clerical housekeeping by all those involved in the aircraft industry. And the supposed purpose of that rigorous clerical housekeeping is to ensure passenger safety. But it is tragic that the clerical activity becomes an end in itself. The entire purpose of the existence of the department is forgotten. There is no employee available to remind everyone of what their essential function is. And so the fact that fuel tanks were pierced on many occasions before the tragic accident is something that is hidden under a paper mountain. And this happens because the dynamic of every employee from the highest rank to the lowest is; to stay in employment.

In private enterprise the dynamic is; you provide quality goods or services, or you go out of business. In public enterprise the dynamic is; to keep money rolling into bank accounts, because their paymaster is trussed up and gagged, and kept out of sight by the socialist interference.

Therefore one would imagine that the socialists, on seeing the failure of their own ideology, would have some respect for private enterprise. Sadly the reverse is true. On recent occasions they have had the temerity to criticise two of the most successful private businesses in the British economy. Those being the oil companies and the supermarkets. Some of those oil companies may have to fund exploration and drilling, and the construction of pipelines to refineries. But all, will have to either do this, or buy the raw material from elsewhere. They also have to pay the cost of storage and distribution. They also have to fund the freehold or leasehold costs of retail sites, and the costs of the administration of the entire business. And then from every thirty seven pounds of turnover one pound goes towards that which sends shock waves through the socialist psyche: profit. And then from every five pounds a British citizen spends on fuel, the same socialists who attacked the oil companies take four pounds in taxation.

So even though the government does no work whatsoever in getting the product to the customer, it takes eighty percent of the revenue generated by the personnel employed by that oil company. And those of us who understand human nature have to sit by and watch the oil companies being shamelessly used as tax collectors, and at the same time facing abuse and threats from the socialist government. But we can be sure of one thing, the Prussian Karl Marx would have been delighted by this behaviour, and the Englishman John Locke would have been astonished and outraged.

They have no difficulty in using those in the market place who are successful, to provide money to them, so that they can continue creating dependants with a socially destructive welfare policy; and continue funding a pathologically destructive health care policy. Since profit can also be described a benefit, no one could ever accuse a socialist government of ever making a profit, since socialism is associated with failure in the same manner as jealousy is associated with enmity.

Accordingly the supermarkets were accused of profiteering. Even though from every fifty pounds of turnover one pound goes towards the socialist's bugbear: profit. All of the supermarkets provide produce of the highest quality at a cost no reasonable person could consider excessive. But yet they had to absorb criticism from people who had never conducted any kind of business large or small themselves. The accusation was that their suppliers were being treated unfairly. But since they were aware that all supermarkets were in competition with each other, they seem to have been suggesting that some should have deliberately damaged their ability to compete in the market place. Or else; they were suggesting that all supermarkets should get together and make a secret deal to pay suppliers more to the detriment of their customers.

Either way they ought to have been invited to go and live in China or North Korea or Zimbabwe, and see what happens to a country when the government intervenes in the market place.

And because the healthy citizen ought to be the norm, and ill health the exception, the service of the provision of food is more vital than a health service. So we ought to imagine a situation just two years after a socialist government nationalised the supermarkets.

Having arrived at the entrance door on Wednesday it was necessary to return again on Thursday. Since the union having negotiated a thirty five hour week meant that the supermarket was closed on Wednesday. The shelves which were formerly replete with good quality fresh produce are now half filled with stale produce. Over by the freezer which hasn't functioned properly for weeks, the flies are vying with the human population for some decaying meat. There is no milk as yet, since the delivery vehicle has broken down on the way to the store. Overhead, most of the light fittings are not working, and one is hanging precariously from the ceiling. The floor space where the fruit and vegetables used to be is given over to a storage area, as this was lost on the first floor, since the manager wanted a larger office. Having considered it safest to buy only tinned produce, there is then a choice of joining one of three very long queues. There are twenty four checkouts but only sufficient staff to occupy three of them. Most of the competent staff have left to get other jobs. Half of the staff still in employment are absent on sick leave. After shuffling towards the checkout for fifteen minutes the cashier who was about to bring the invalidation to an end, gets up and goes to lunch. Some minutes later she is replaced by someone whose countenance betrays the fact that her morale has got no further to descend. When the cost of the goods are totalled she adds an extortionate amount for the use of the car park. The attitude is; "you ought to be grateful we provide you with any kind of service at all." Just like the attitude in the Marxist health service.

And it is useful to investigate some of the less obvious reasons why this situation can come about. And one of those unfortunately seems to be, that the provision of health care has become an emotive issue. Even though there seems to be no logical reason why somebody who goes to university and absorbs numerous facts and regurgitates them under examination conditions should be worthy of any more respect than a bricklayer, carpenter or tailor, there appears to be chronic subordination on the part of the average person towards doctors. And the explanation would appear to be that the patient believes that if he does not ingratiate himself with the doctor the information he has about the causes of ill health will be withheld.

In other words he believes the doctor has a choice whether he does his job or not. The patient who attends with a medical problem is saying; "You know so much, I know so little. I am at your mercy." And however sporadic this may have been prior to the nationalisation of the health service it is now, due to the infantilisation of the electorate quite widespread.

So the provision of this service seems to be transmitted via goodwill alone. And when such enormous power is vested in another; is it any wonder that doctors are unwilling to question their own judgement or ability? They haven't demanded that power but they have acquired it by default. And even though most would probably accept that the patient is better placed to know precisely what brings about fluctuations in their state of health; it is not their style to try to engender any kind of introspection. And so the less the patient knows about what may be necessary to ensure the maintenance of health, the greater the emotional bond between himself and the doctor. The thought that he should be paid like the carpenter or tailor for providing a service is quite frightening for such a person. It is a kind of child-adult relationship where the sweets are often dispensed in tablet form, from a bottle.

While the importance of the presence or absence of empathy has been emphasised earlier with regard to much of human behaviour, the same empathy leads to thoughts and beliefs which are not entirely rational.

Recently an editor of a daily newspaper saw fit to use an entire front page with a photograph of a very young baby. Following a natural disaster in Mozambique this baby had been plucked to safety by rescuers in a helicopter from a neighbouring country. And in order for the editor to do this he must have believed this would inspire more sales of his newspaper. And he was probably right. But we must ask how could the survival of one baby thousands of miles away inspire any Briton to buy a newspaper? Were they very happy that with a world population of over six billion one more baby survived? And if they were happy that the world's population was greater by one than it otherwise might have been; why would they go to bed that night and actually ensure that they did not have any, or any more, babies themselves? Could they have a higher regard for a baby born thousands of miles away than they could for their own? Surely that would not make genetic or biological sense. No. The real reason is that they found the whole event very gratifying, because they felt that if they were a tiny little helpless baby in a tree they would like someone to come along and rescue them.

But we can be sure that if the person rescued was a fifty-nine year old man, he would not be on the front page of the newspaper. So why do we have a greater fondness for babies than fifty-nine year olds? Surely fifty-nine year olds are more interesting since the baby cannot speak. Why does it not make more sense for a politician to kiss those who can vote, rather than babies who can't? Does the explanation lie in the fact that adults have a fondness for all babies because babies are not capable of adversely affecting them in any way? And we do not have the same fondness for all fifty nine year olds because they might well have adversely affected us in some way. When two murders are committed; one of a six year old girl, and one of a twenty eight year old man, we can see the contrasting reactions to both.

The girl having been strangled; and the man having been fatally stabbed in an attempted street robbery. The girl's parents and older brother are grief stricken. The man's wife and three young children are grief stricken. But the public do not consider the man's death is in any way as heinous as the girl's death. The three members of the girl's family are not dependent on her and their sadness will lessen in time. The sadness of the man's wife will lessen in time. But the three children will no longer have the encouragement, security, stability, love and affection they once had. The loss of their father will adversely affect their psychological well-being. And when the police arrest suspects for both crimes the reaction of grown ups outside the respective courts is very different.

Outside one, many men and women wait for a long time to be able to shout abuse and threats as the suspect is driven in. Their demeanour suggests that they would tear the suspect apart with their bare hands given the opportunity. Outside the other court as the suspect is driven in: nothing. Does this mean that they consider that the man was fair game and the girl was not? Or could it be that the adults who have become so emotionally involved have never been adversely affected by a six year old girl? And, they therefore consider it was far more evil to take the life of a six year old girl than a twenty eight year old man. We have to conclude that no logic can be observed in the reaction to both incidents.

The consequences of both killings are not considered. The resulting behaviour of others is governed by emotion. And it can be reasonably stated that the more emotion is involved in any situation the less intelligence is involved. But it can be clearly seen that events surrounding babies and young children have a greater impact on the emotions of some grown ups than events surrounding other members of the population. And the manner in which those grown ups are moved to act is in empathising with a baby in a tree, or in their desire for vengeance. But just as we observe an upsurge in emotion in certain people, we observe a similar factor of inconsistency. When they wait outside a courthouse waiting to vent their anger, they know that they are perfectly safe. They know that there are barriers and many police between themselves and the despised suspect. But when a parent or parents systematically abuse their own children necessitating their removal from their own premises; those very same people stay very quiet indeed.

Should they meet a couple in the street whose child has been removed from them for its own safety, we can be sure they would not issue any kind of abuse of threats; without the barriers and the police there to protect them. For there is no censure whatsoever by the people for those who take children into the world without the means to adequately provide for them. On the contrary: they applaud a politician who takes more and more taxation to give to the parents of those 'deprived' children. And he in his turn is motivated by his awareness of the displaced concern for the welfare of babies and children in the general population. But even if we were not aware of his real motives, why would the handing over of other people's taxes induce someone to care for their own children, who was not doing so prior to his involvement? After all, he has no jurisdiction over how the money is spent.

But in an adult nation under adult government there would be no need for the interference of politicians in the area of child care. There would be an inescapable expectation of all parents to take full responsibility for the welfare of their own children. And it is indicative, by the extent of government involvement in this area, that no such expectation exists in this society. But just as the Marxist health service is an emotive issue, so too is the phrase 'childhood poverty'. But instead of a government asking; how can we get more taxes, the proper question would be; who are the parents? If there are children living in poverty it is the responsibility of just two people. And when a government gets involved in making a pretence at rectifying a problem, it does so by using force. It uses force to raise more revenue through taxation. So people who had no part to play in the creation of the problem are forced to provide the solution. Even though it will never be anything other than a fictitious solution. For it is rarely, if ever, money that is in short supply, but; poverty of love and affection. And that will not be altered one iota by increased benefits.

So when we are aware that people are motivated to act because of an emotional feeling, it is easy to see how many people allow themselves to be persuaded by an irrational ideology. For if people do not question that which ought to be questioned, the dishonest may be accepted as the truth. And when people are carried along by an ideology, given enough time, some will find it impossible to escape.

I speak of the one and a half million drug addicts created by the Marxist health service. Those people cannot escape. The method of ensuring they were locked into the socialist ideology was via tonnes of benzodiazepines. Most of those products carried recommendations from the manufacturer that they be prescribed for a short period to assist a patient over some brief anxiety. But they were prescribed month after month, year after year, decade after decade. And hence a vast number became addicted. This is just one example of the damage caused by the interference of a third party in the market place. This situation came about because of the absence of rational interruption on behalf of the first or second party.

The patient did not stop to consider if it was such a good idea to continue with the drugs. If they were not being given out free this might have happened. If the patient had to pay their own money, they may have stopped and wondered if they were really worth it; if they really needed them at all. But because they were free, they took advantage of the freeness as people are wont to do. The patient also believed that the doctor had the self-interest of the patient in mind. He had also heard politicians talking about their concern for the provision of good health care and could not believe that the service of which they spoke could render patients more unwell than if they were to avoid the service entirely.

As for the doctor, he did not have to pay for the drug either and had no motivation to stop prescribing it. The patient may return to his surgery once in a while complaining about further anxiety; but all he has to do then is strengthen the dose; until a time in the future when they return again. This makes his job very easy, he doesn't have to do any real work; it is easier to mask the symptoms than discover the cause. He knows he is involved in an absurd system, which eight out of ten of his predecessors in 1948 tried to explain to the politicians of the day.

But the doctors were induced into the system by a mechanism of which Marx would have been proud, when all connection was broken between work done and remuneration received. So the taxpayer funds a system which, on the one hand, enables a state employee to draw a salary without doing their job; and on the other hand, adversely affects the health of many citizens despite the supposed purpose being the opposite. This then is the nature of socialism.

But the political fallout from such a situation is very beneficial. For we can easily empathise with the situation of the drug addict at election time. In reality they are faced with two possibilities. There is the possibility of a party coming to power with a policy of reducing public expenditure and the possibility of a party coming to power with a policy of increasing public expenditure. And they know that if they vote for the latter the continued funding of their drugs is guaranteed. And the thought that the former may threaten the open-ended expenditure on drugs would cause further anxiety. Therefore, as has already been said, people vote for a party in their own self-interest, no matter how minute that self-interest may be; and because of this fact, the drug addicts are in the iron grip of the socialists. And since no party in Britain could ever have come to power if there had been a shift of allegiance of one million five hundred thousand votes, this is the clearest contamination of democracy there can be. Those people are not voting against a laissez-faire society, or for a socialist society; they are voting to retain funding of the drugs on which they have become so reliant.

But if any citizen in 1930 was feeling overburdened by the pressure of life, they would not go to a doctor, they would talk to friends or relatives and be offered true and beneficial assistance. They would be offered valuable assistance because it would be in the self-interest of those people to help their relative or friend. But when a doctor is working particularly under a Marxist system, it is not in his self-interest to offer valuable assistance to anybody.

For we ought to be very clear about the fact; that a student goes on to study medicine, and become a doctor, because they know that in so doing, they will be able to command a higher salary in the market place than a cobbler. If anybody believes that a man or woman becomes a doctor with the primary aim of curing the sick; then they are deluding themselves. Some may obtain considerable job satisfaction from time to time because of their ability to cure the sick, but it is the same satisfaction the lawyer may obtain from winning a court case. And just as lawyers need people to break the law, doctors need people who have to rely on them for assistance. If everybody was in perfect health, doctors would have to find other jobs.

And the person above; advised by their relative or friend to think differently about life's challenges, would in the future be better able to cope with a fresh challenge. But even if they were not aware that thought processes were the fundamental cause of the problem, whatever they were to advise, would be better than resorting to drugs. Because drugs cannot change thought processes, they can only subdue the neurological response to thought process. And when the next challenge comes along the drug assisted person will be less well able to cope than the first time.

And when we compare the situation when there was no third party in existence to be invited in, and when the third party was in existence, we have a microcosm of all socialist interference and failure. For what the socialists did in 1948 was to say to the friends and relatives; "Step aside, we can handle this. We know best". And they did this for the purpose of gaining power over people's lives. And the presence or absence of power is the most important factor in why all communism and all socialism must fail.

From the first days on this planet when our distant ancestors began to trade in goods or services there has been a perfect equilibrium between the suppliers of those goods and services and the recipients of those goods or services. If there was a need or desire for something and it was met by another, there was mutual exploitation and both parties had to be in agreement with that exploitation or no trading occurred. It was entirely in the self-interest of both parties that the exchange should take place. One party retained the power to decide exactly what quantity of goods he was prepared to offer for other goods or services. And the second party retained the power to accept or reject or negotiate the deal. Then in much more recent times with the advent of money, the situation became even more clearly defined with values of a quarter of a penny deciding the acceptance or rejection of the deal. And whether it was money that was being exchanged or gold or diamonds or silk or spices, trade led to the greatest advance in civilisation. And whatever the scale of the trade, it was conducted between individuals where either party had the power to say yes or no to the deal.

But then less than one hundred years ago significant numbers of people were motivated to believe; in their own self-interest that this perfect equilibrium ought to be smashed; and the power of the two parties be wrestled from them and vested in a third party. And hence the situation remains in the Marxist health service; where the self-interest and the power is removed from the service provider and the patient. And when the power is removed from both parties, and all equilibrium destroyed, nobody ought to be surprised when the resulting service is disastrous. For those in possession of a fraudulent ideology are not going to change the most powerful determining factor in all evolution; the self-interest of the individual organism.

The doctor sitting in his surgery talking to his patient, has no connection with that patient. He can either regard the patient as a nuisance or he can decide to offer some real assistance depending on how he is disposed on the day. Whatever he decides to do, it will have no impact one way or another on his salary. Should he be someone who is competent and useful he is treated in the same way by his employer as those who are incompetent and useless. Not only is this the case but the employer has no knowledge whatsoever regarding the identity of the competent or incompetent. The patient sitting in his surgery who has visited seven times in the last year has the same importance for him as the name of a person on a piece of paper, who has not spoken to him for five years. He gets the same income because of the existence of the two human beings. His self-interest is served simply by being a doctor, and following the diktats of the remote health department. His self-interest cannot be served by any behaviour whatever within the remit of the job description. So he goes through the motions, as taxpayer's money flows into his bank account. He has no power to promote his self-interest other than to remain as someone who can be called a doctor. The patient also is entirely disempowered by the socialist state; which takes his money by force and thereby smashes the equilibrium that existed between service provider and customer from the very beginning of all such human interaction.

Whereas the bricklayer, carpenter and tailor have a vested interest in being competent in their job, and providing a good service, the state employed doctor has no such impetus. The only possibility of his being so motivated would be if the patient had the power to withdraw their custom following incompetence. But the patient has no such power; only customers have power.

Only when the incompetent doctor sees the prospect of having to sell his car, move to a smaller house, or abandon foreign holidays, would he be motivated to provide a quality service. And this would only happen if dissatisfied customers started to take their money elsewhere. And just as the law on the preservation of energy exists, so does the law on the preservation of power. And the combined power that ought to rightfully reside in the hands of customers, has been wrestled from them by the socialists, to be used at election time to buy political power for themselves.

Many decades ago when I was fourteen and I first heard that phrase, inveigling the incarnation of indolence: 'from each according to their ability to each according to their need', I immediately considered it the most absurd nonsense I had ever heard. And what is hard to understand, is that people who have lived much longer and have mounting evidence year after year that socialism fails, still would violently disagree with my early assessment. And it fails because the ideology is contrary to nature itself.

The fact is that people will not work for the state as they would work for themselves. It is not in their self-interest to work for the state. It is in their self-interest to work for themselves. Since there is no altruism, people will not work to benefit other citizens, they will work to benefit themselves. And it is curious that an ideology spawned from the pre-eminence of enmity and the self-interest of those driving socialism, should be expected to thrive in conditions where there is expected to be the entire absence of enmity and self-interest . And of course, we see that it never thrives. On the contrary, it destroys nations and economies slowly but surely. Because, it is a denial of nature, and an obstruction of the life force, it leads to devastating failure. Whereas in the most capitalist economies where nature is unimpeded they experience spectacular success.

9. On Education

When politicians pontificate about education the unmistakable impression is that it is something like lemon juice which ought to be provided in a glass, to someone suffering from scurvy. And just as the spending of more public money on lemon juice would give rise to fewer and fewer persons suffering from scurvy; the spending of more money on education would lead to a better educated young population. But lemon juice is a product and education is an enabling service. And while everyone suffering from a disease would have an interest in availing of the cure, everyone clearly does not have an interest in availing of the enabling service of education. Many do, if education could be expressed in liquid terms, take the glass from the teacher and defiantly throw the contents onto the ground before them.

Then the socialists on seeing this behaviour, suggest that if the contents were to cost a great deal more money, then perhaps the young person may drink it. But what they do not want to understand is that like all services in human life, it must be driven by need. And while nobody can expect that need to be understood by young persons; the need must be a parental need. And judging from the number of semi-literates leaving the system, it is obvious that many parents have had no need of such a service. And we must ask how a situation has come about where vast public funds are spent on a service where many are seen to have no need.

Prior to any states' involvement in any education system young persons were taught in various ways. Some were taught by their own parents until they were old enough to teach themselves. Some were taught by various religious sects, usually for the purposes of advancing their own creed; and some were taught by lay professionals, whose parents bought the service as they would any other. And the one factor common to all of those so taught was a determination on behalf of their parents that they should be educated. They saw that it was in their own self-interest to ensure their offspring were better equipped to compete in the market place. And in being better equipped they would be able to go on to command higher earnings than others; and thus be able to enjoy a better quality of life than perhaps their parents. This is a natural aspiration. And it is not just because of the love and affection that ought to exist, but because of the genetic bond between parent and offspring. Since if an individual is enabled to compete more effectively than others, then they can also be more selective in their choice of mate, making it more likely that they will produce strong healthy grandchildren for their parents. And this process of enabling is as much part of evolution as the activity of all the myriad life forms that assist their young to survive. But this enabling would never arise if man were not capable of projecting his thoughts into the future. Just as he lives in a competitive world, he can by virtue of his imagination feel quite certain that his children will also live in a competitive world. And knowing this, he sets about furnishing them with as much assistance to survive in that world as he can.

But while it is patently obvious that this is a natural aspiration by most parents, it is also equally obvious that it is not a universal aspiration. Some parents have little or no regard for their children's future, which usually stems from them having little or no regard for themselves. And while some stretch every nerve and sinew to assist their children; while others do nothing, it only serves to highlight the fact that there is no uniformity in human life. Not only is there no uniformity in human life, there is no uniformity throughout nature. Should there have been uniformity, there would have been no evolution. And should there have been no evolution there would be no group of people to feel so inadequate and threatened when exposed to the competitive process. And therefore those who aspire towards equality and uniformity are engaged in the negation of that force which gave rise to their very being. They are incapable of accepting difference. And thus a situation arises under government that would not arise under natural law.

The government, which is some people, try to provide a service for some other people who do not want the service. Therefore if they do not want the service, it is of no value to them, and they would not be prepared to contribute any money towards the service. This situation could not pertain under natural law, but exists under government interference. If no self-interest is served no relationship of whatever kind can exist between two individuals. And the result of the forced maintenance of the relationship is the wasting of other people's money. A situation which has become more acute in recent times.

Approximately midway through the twentieth century there was a government determination that there ought to be 'free secondary education for all'. For a long time prior to this there had been close collaboration between politicians of all parties, and the person responsible for the relevant bill giving rise to this, was obviously influenced in his terminology by socialist attitudes. Because there had been continual progress in the expansion of educational facilities in the previous one hundred years, in announcing the next stage of expansion he ought to have had the good sense to use the phrase; 'taxation assisted secondary education for all', instead. In knowing, as he ought to have, that people are disposed to abuse that which is free, the use of the phrase, was, at best negligent. Especially given that it was at variance with the truth. Prior to his remark, close on forty per cent of those entering universities in England and Wales were of the elementary and grant-aided secondary school origin; and nobody considered using the phrase, 'free secondary education' for the children of parents who value the service in their regard. Because free it is not, now, and never was. But whatever deleterious impact the use of such a misleading word had on the attitude of some parents, it was as nothing in comparison to the destructive social policy enacted later.

And that social policy says:

"We in the government give you, dear citizen, total freedom to do whatever you like; you do not have to be responsible for any aspect of your life, we undertake to unconditionally underwrite the provision of all of your needs."

And what better method could one devise to undermine an education system?

For any service to exist in human life there has to be a purpose for that service. Originally it was for the purpose of enabling children to compete more effectively in the market place. Then governments saw that the education of its people was in the national interest. And this was in response to a changing world. As politicians were elected to serve the interests of their nation they saw that investment in education would serve those interests in the same way as investment in infrastructure. They saw that their nation was becoming ever more a trading nation and the better educated a population, the better those trading interests would be served. They saw that their nation was in competition with other nations and to allow their own to be hampered by lack of expertise or knowledge would be negligent.

And this situation continued until the acerbic enmity of the socialists made education an internal political battleground. Should they have been governed by rational thought they would not have been capable of doing this. For presumably they ought to have known that the duty of an elected politician in government is to serve the interests of the nation. And they also ought to have known that attacking any educational institution either verbally or through policy was not serving the interests of their nation. But, had they been able to find the resources, through an improved economy, to ensure that the children of just one hundred more citizens had a higher standard of education, then that would have been in the national interest. But since socialists have always adversely affected the economy they were not capable of doing this. Instead they set about destruction rather than construction. And they hoped that in the ensuing mess nobody would be able to identify how much damage they had done.

And that destruction was motivated by a drive towards uniformity. A drive towards the puerile attempt to obliterate individual difference. Like their view of 'the rich' or 'the poor' or their convenient rigidity of class demarcation they saw school children as an amorphous mass of human tissue that had no individuality; and the parents who produced the amorphous mass had no widely different beliefs in the value or necessity of

190

education. But above all like every other area of socialist intervention in human life they wanted control. For control permits manipulation, and manipulation produces votes. And unless they were prepared to pass laws blatantly contravening human rights their control could not extend to the public schools. They were not prepared to make it unlawful for one man to provide a service for another at an agreed price. They didn't like the public schools, but they were not nearly so annoyed by them as they were the grammar schools.

Some observers have been a little surprised by this; but in the light of understanding the socialist mentality it is not surprising. We know that the socialist is motivated by jealousy and greed and even though they may have been jealous of those who could send their children to public schools, they were not contributing to those public schools. They were, however, contributing to grammar schools. And because they were paying money towards something which was going to benefit other people's children they became very angry indeed. An articulation of their attitude was; "If I'm paying money towards this; I'm damned sure that someone else's son, whom I despise, because he may be cleverer than my son, is not going to get an advantage from it, so I would rather destroy it." And they would not have been wrong in the comparison of their sons. For there can be no doubt that a child brought up in a home where there is love and positivity will be able to think more clearly than a child brought up in a home where there is enmity and negativity. And the test at eleven that determined selection for grammar schools was a test of an ability to think clearly. And just as the children of non-socialists were likely to gain entry to grammar schools because of their ability to think clearly, so too the socialists continued with their destructive policies because of their own inability to think clearly.

A mature response from politicians who were concerned with the interests of the nation would have been to build more grammar schools and grade them one to four or whatever grading spread was necessary in a particular area, and provide an appropriate range of subjects. And just as footballers who play in second and third division teams do not need psychological counselling every week, neither would eleven year old children. But for their own political purposes the socialists blubbered and objected repeatedly about the attendant failure that resulted from not gaining admittance to a grammar school. But it is probably the case that no eleven year old was ever perturbed for very long about not passing any examination. That is if they were left to their own devices; but they may well have been perturbed, if they had to shoulder the angst of the grown up children they had as parents; who wanted to live their own lives again, through their children.

If on any one day an eleven year old does not give sufficient correct answers to another's questions and does not pass an examination then that is all that has happened. It does not in any way whatsoever determine the life of that person. The route to the highest level of academic achievement is not blocked, and never was by the non attendance at grammar school. The only failure was the failure of parents to understand that nobody can determine another's destiny. But as has been stated earlier socialists feel powerless, and feel themselves, as Marx did, to be victims of other people's decisions. And their belief that somebody correcting an eleven year old's examination paper had power over their lives led to their growing to despise those people.

Hence they set about closing grammar schools and replacing them with comprehensive schools. In that way they could ensure that nobody had the power to make them feel bad. Even though the passing or not passing an examination on the part of their child had no such power, they convinced themselves that the matter was a fitting subject for feeling bad. And hence they abolished the necessity for entrance examinations and thus abolished the possibility of their feeling bad. So all pupils were admitted to comprehensive schools and placed in classes with widely varying abilities. Even the socialists didn't have the power to alter the very obvious fact that children of a similar age differ greatly in ability. And when some of those began to show signs that they were able to understand what was being taught, they incurred teasing and ridicule from those who felt bad because they didn't know as much as someone else. And soon the bullying group forced the more able to fall into line. But if the sensibilities of the socialist psyche were assuaged then what did it matter if standards fell? When enmity is allowed free reign, there has to be a consequence somewhere. But it was not only socialist politicians who were trying to enforce uniformity on their own. They were ably assisted by many teachers and educationalists of the day. And they also had become socialists for the reasons given in an earlier section.

Because they felt they were pioneers in the shaping of a brave new world, they had to abandon the old teaching methods which they considered corrupt and divisive. And new methods in primary schools had to be used which would prevent any pupil appearing too clever and making the others feel bad. So whole class teaching had to be ended in the interests of egalitarianism. So the teacher visited small groups from time to time who had been working together as a 'team'. And anything that was contributed was a team effort. The individual must not be allowed to shine. And the rationale for those new methods was that it would assist the social development of the child. But one wonders if any parent would ever pay for the service of education, because of their belief that their child was in need of social development.

Those who believed that they had a legitimate concern in this area ought to have led them to instruct children how to eat and drink. For socialisation is governed by the determination for the satisfaction of needs; and the path of their social development was overwhelmingly determined by what happened in their earlier years. Perhaps they believed that before socialism the world was somehow socially deficient. Perhaps they felt that man being a social animal was insufficiently a social animal. Perhaps they hoped to improve on nature. But they would have done well to reflect on the fact that the most horrific slaughter has occurred on this planet since the advent of socialism. But they still felt, while in possession of an ideology that is rooted in an enmity of others, that they had a part to play in the social development of children.

And because of this and other so called progressive methods, time that ought to have been spent in explaining, clarifying, instructing, informing, guiding and inspiring those in their charge to think for themselves, was lost. But this was a time when the omnicompetent socialist state had lulled people into a kind of hypnotic condition, where the automatic belief was that 'the government knows best'. And it took decades for the failed progressive methods, and the drive towards uniformity, to reveal just how damaging they had been. When employers began to complain that they were being sent people who could hardly read or write, some politicians thought it was time for a review of methods. And then when it became possible to compare the performance of one school with another the extent of the difference gave cause for concern. But the most interesting discovery provided by the new mechanism, was that there was no qualitative relationship between the amount of money spent on a pupil's education, and their resultant achievement. This ought to have had some impact on at least one political party, which has a persistent puerile mantra suggesting that there must be a qualitative relationship between the two. But no impact was made; providing us with the clearest insight into how much logic is brought to bear on British politics. Not only was there no link, but in some areas of significantly lower spending, there resulted significantly higher achievement. But then the most reliable time honoured, trusted riposte by the socialists in defending their high spending areas with poor achievement is; 'but these are deprived areas'. This will silence the critics. This will make them stash their statistics away. But the people in those 'deprived areas' are not deprived of multi-faceted music systems, state of the art recording devices, numerous television channels, money for gambling, tobacco and alcohol; they are just deprived.

They are deprived because they have accepted the socialists' sop. Deprived of ambition for personal advancement. Deprived of the need for restraint. Deprived of the need to take risks, that lead to wisdom. Deprived of the evolutionary authenticity of being in a market society. Deprived of any need to be resolute, shrewd, determined or disciplined. Deprived of the ability to control their own lives. Deprived of any possible sense of achievement. Deprived of the need for a life plan. Deprived of any interest in self reliance. But most importantly of all; deprived of any incentive to encourage their children to learn. All their deprivation results from socialist ideology, and their absurd destructive social policy. And even though, as much money is spent on their education as some private day schools, they will leave the education system with the kind of qualifications that will ensure they have little choice but to rely on taxpayers for their needs, and remain like their parents; pawns in the socialist game.

And when things go badly in education the government can always fund a 'report' to find out the cause. This will keep critics at bay for a while, and employ more civil servants. And after one such report the major finding regarding the educational development of any child was:

"that the most vital factor in a child's home was the attitude to school, and all that went on there, of its mother and father: 'The interested parent has the interested child'."

It may seem odd that it required the expenditure of taxpayer's money for someone to discover that which must have been patently obvious to every adult. But even so, no matter how much that fact may be highlighted, no attitudes will ever change because of the present social policy. For why should someone who is relying on others for all of their needs encourage their children to do otherwise? If they considered that there was something unacceptable about it, then it wouldn't be happening. They know the future for their children is secured whether literate or illiterate. And since it is more difficult to learn than not to learn; the television programme becomes a more attractive proposition than anything to do with education.

If there were the prospect of suffering some serious disadvantage in future because of an inadequate education, then there would be the motivation to make use of the service. But since there is no prospect of this happening, there is no motivation. The cruelest irony is that, when they in their turn are provided with accommodation, they will have a higher disposable income for a decade or more, than some student who rigorously followed through to the highest qualifications and then set about acquiring their own accommodation in the market place. It would of course, be a cruel irony under natural law; but under socialist law, it is the modus operandi that drives the conveyor belt of socialist votes.

But concerns over the success or failure within an education system are only relevant because of the percentage of those who fail that are likely to become dependant on taxpayers for their needs. Otherwise it ought to remain an entirely personal matter. But because education is not consumer led it suffers from the twin distortions of, on the one hand, being undermined by the state itself, and on the other, of inordinate reverence being attached to academic achievement. For academic achievement is only precisely that. It is only an indicator that someone may have the ability to fulfil the necessary function in any particular area of employment. But indicators are no guarantee of future merit. It does not mean that the person is capable of doing anything of value. And when it is found that the person is not capable of doing anything of value, the time between discovery and their being relieved of their duties ought to be measured in hours rather than days.

Unfortunately however, in the interests of a more vibrant economy, this does not happen often enough in the private sector; and rarely if ever in the public sector. There, responsibility for ineptitude is rarely accepted. Since we know that the primary function of all, is to remain in employment, the attitude is; if you question the ability of one of us, you question the ability of all of us. Therefore prevarication, cover-up and obfuscation ensues. Those who become employed there, use academic achievement as a kind of body armour to protect them for ever. But it bears no direct relationship to merit. And there may well be individuals in society who had spurned all that academia had to offer and may be able to carry out the functions of some person of high academic achievement far more effectively. But they will never attain the position. One; because the inept person will remain in their position, and two, because they are not able to provide the necessary indication that they could do the job. The only thing that academic achievement provides is an externally performed function of sifting, which allows a prospective employer to make a judgement in the most time efficient manner.

But when that indication is provided, and it later transpires that ability in practise falls far short of expectation, employment law has ensured that the disparity between the two is solidly bridged. And that employment law is one of the factors that contributes to the inordinate reverence for academic achievement. For in a true meritocracy it would not be possible for those who are incapable to remain in their positions. And should there be evidence available to all that those who had provided the necessary indication; were relieved of their duties immediately on discovery of their inability; then reverance for academic achievement would fall to its appropriate level. But the state's interference causes many dangerous distortions in human life.

The civil servants controlling education can change the name of some educational institutions, and call them universities or change an examination acronym here or an acronym there for the sake of some imaginary improvement. But what matters greatly is what kind of people are leaving those institutions at the end of their courses. What are they capable of doing? All the evidence seems to be that there is creeping shoddiness in every profession. Could it be the case that once the certificate is obtained, and they are under the protection of employment law, their work is done? They can now relax. Are there no lessons to be learned from the fact that, most of the industrial, entrepreneurial and creative geniuses are those who left the education system prematurely? They were not able to rely on some academic achievement to induce someone else to value them; they valued themselves, and went on to greatness. And while necessity is the mother of invention, the social policy makes it less likely that individuals such as those will emerge in the future.

But those who are involved in a profession where their shoddiness is verifiable as the outcome of some activity are in a sense the unfortunate ones. For there are many professions where there is no observable outcome of any activity. They are entirely safe. For example, the case of the educational psychologist.

She is sitting at a distance, observing the activities in a classroom of seven year olds, where some of them have; 'behavioural problems'. She pays particular attention to one boy who is particularly disruptive. But no matter how many notes she makes or how much analysis of his interactions she may do, she will not make an iota of difference to this boy's life. And at the end of the year when she has banked her salary, no one will question her achievement. This boy's life and the lives of his two older sisters, began to change when he was less than three years of age. At that time his mother began a relationship with another man and the ensueing conflict was resolved when the divorce law ensured her husband was removed from his home.

When the relationship soon ended she proceeded to raise the children on her own. Her son's behaviour changed gradually from minor misbehaviour to more serious misbehaviour. Then he refused to go to bed until everyone else went to bed. He acquired the habit of pulling his sisters hair and making them cry. He was now becoming very powerful. At four and a half he refused to eat his food. His mother would sit at the table with him and try to persuade him to eat. Sometimes he just pushed the food onto the floor. She used all kinds of bribery and persuasion but he would only eat certain kinds of foods at a time of his choosing. At five and a half he had the power to manipulate his mother totally.

And all he ever wanted from the outset of his minor misbehaviour was for some adult to provide him with a sense of security. But there was no adult in the house, there was just a grown-up. The state had removed the adult. All it would have taken in the early stages was a look, or a word from an adult to modify his early egocentrism. With each act of defiance he was crying out ever louder for someone to assure him in his small vulnerable state that he did not have the power to control everybody. But his cry was never answered. He became more and more insecure. He could not come to terms with a world where a little boy like him had the power to manipulate everybody else. And now in the classroom his manic, boisterous unruly behaviour reflects his insecurity. As he gets bigger and stronger his unruly behaviour continues until one day he is shouting abuse at the wardens in a young offenders institution.

And those who passed the laws which led to his father being ousted from his life will not see that they have been party to an act of social sabotage. They passed a law which allowed one party to take legal action to dissolve a marriage, and be virtually certain of gaining hugely from the exercise. And if they did not know that such a law would lead to a rapid escalation in the break up of families; then they ought not to have been on the fringes of a parish council meeting; let alone in the parliament of a nation state. They had no wisdom, no understanding of human nature, and no understanding of the dynamics regarding the pair bonding process between a man and a woman. And the dynamic of that pair bonding is so complex and delicate that it can never be assisted by the bludgeoning force of state law.

For two people with unique psychological profiles had chosen each other because of their emotional similarly, making conflict practically inevitable from time to time. And then when that conflict does arise the availability of partisan assistance to one parent, speeds the destruction of the family unit which would not occur under other circumstances. Even if both parties wished to live separate lives when their son was three years of age, the involvement of both extended families would have led to a civilised arrangement where their son would not have suffered. Instead, the state made a minor skirmish into an all out war, greatly benefiting two lawyers, and damaging the lives of three children. And now a civil servant sits making notes about this boy's activities, drawing her salary from the state: the same state that caused his 'behavioural problems'.

But if we forget the purpose of high taxation and the control it brings, we may well find ourselves asking if the politicians who administer over this state of affairs are deliberately refusing to see, or cannot see, the damaging consequences of their laws.

In education, as in every other service there ought to be multi-tier provision, reflecting the multi-tier level of respect and need for the service by parents and their children. And at the lowest tier, would be all those pupils who had shown no interest whatever in acquiring an education, from the higher tiers. This would be a building where those pupils would spend the period of the normal school day. There would be no pretence of teaching them. Those in charge would have no other function than to provide assistance if requested and ensure health and safety. There would be no exclusions allowing pupils to attend amusement arcades or engage in petty crime. After two weeks they would have the option of requesting to return to education or staying where they were. Should they return and a teacher had to spend any time dealing with their disrespectful, undisciplined, disruptive behaviour, then they would be returned to the secure building and wait four weeks before having the option of requesting to return. There could no longer be the continuing insult to the teaching profession in expecting teachers to teach the unteachable. Should they no longer be invalidated the quality teachers who have left the profession may return. But there could be no greater measure taken to improve educational standards than the abandonment of the absurd and destructive social policy.

But like all the other areas of interference in the market place, it is the basis of socialist ideology, and will not be changed by them. However, what we will see more of, is suggestions by the person in overall command of the education system, that parents of undisciplined children be forced to attend parenting classes. And more suggestions that civil servants from education authorities should apply to magistrates for orders which would force parents to curb their children's unruliness. And more suggestions that parents be obliged to attend coaching sessions on discipline. Sadly however, the implication of those suggestions are, the further penalisation of responsible disciplined citizens, to find the taxes to pay the people entrusted with the task of going through the motions of making undisciplined parents become disciplined. For the effort is futile.

For the socialist state in removing all need for personal discipline, or personal responsibility, or personal restraint, has taught people how to behave. Undisciplined parents raise undisciplined children as night follows day. And therefore the duty of civilised governments directed by adult citizens is to ensure no laws or policies reward irresponsible behaviour. And since we do not have that civilised government now, or did not have thirty five years ago when current problems were created, we will undoubtedly hear further inane suggestions in the future. Inane suggestions; because if people do not understand the cause of the problem, they can never arrive at the solution.

10. On Racism

In his quest for truth in the field of human behaviour, David Hume spoke repeatedly about sympathy. And that sympathy, was not just a compassionate feeling we had for someone in some kind of difficulty.   For him, sympathy was a principle of communication. We get some measure of his view when he said:

"No quality of human nature is more remarkable both in itself and in its consequences than that propensity we have to sympathise with others, and to receive by communication their inclinations and sentiments, however different from, or even contrary to our own."

He saw that sympathy was exactly correspondent to the operations of our understanding;   and that our esteem of any aspect of another, good or bad, can only come to us through sympathy. And also worthy of noting, especially under this topic; from the man who had said that reason serves as the eyes and ears of the passions;   from this reflection of impressions and identity of ideas, the passion arises.

Sympathy he saw as nothing but the conversion of an idea into an impression by the force of imagination. He went on to say that the idea, or rather impression of ourselves, is always intimately present with us and that it is not possible to imagine; since our consciousness gives us such a lively conception of our own person, any means of going beyond ourselves. He reflected that nature had preserved a great resemblance among all human creatures and that we never comment on any passion or principle in others that we will not find in ourselves in some degree. And just as the body is similar, so too is the fabric of the mind. The shape and size may differ, but the structure and composition are in general the same. And he felt that this resemblance very much contributed to make us enter into the sentiments of others. When he implies that this very remarkable sympathy compels us to be social beings, it is clear his view of the word sympathy differs from the conventional. And when we note his other references, we have to agree that, as often as not, the word we use today would be more fitting.

"Sympathy being nothing but a lively idea converted into an impression, it is evident that in considering the future possible or probable condition of any person, we may enter into it with so vivid a conception as to make it our own concern; and by that means be sensible of pains and pleasures, which neither belong to ourselves, nor at the present instant have any real existence."

But he says it is impossible for us to extend this sympathy without being aided by some circumstance in the present, which strikes upon us in a lively manner and he says:

"By means of this lively notion I am interested in them; take part with them; and feel a sympathetic motion in my breast, comparable to whatever I imagine in his."

There can be little doubt, because of the use of the phrase; entering into, making his own, and being sensible of pains and pleasures; that he was doing what we would regard today as empathising. And what he regarded as his lively notion in the above quotation was his empathy.

He alludes to being shown around a dwelling by the owner who is so proud of its convenient construction and he says:

"We enter into his interest by the force of imagination, and feel the same satisfaction, that the objects naturally occasion in him."

And having reached this point with imagination and empathy it is somewhat remarkable that Hume did not take the matter to its further stages. When he said that we blame a father for neglecting his child, and then questioned why this should be. He answered that it showed a want of natural affection, which is a duty of every parent. But his next reasonable question could have been: Why should it bother him that someone else was lacking in natural affection if it was not affecting him? But he did not ask. For if he did, he would have discovered that he was empathising with the neglected child and therefore was moved to blame the father. Had he applied the same rigour to this area as he did to, for example, the infinite divisibility of our ideas of space and time, he would not have been content with the somewhat feeble answer that someone else was lacking in natural affection. In other areas; painstakingly, and with great honesty he left few stones unturned in looking to the source of our idea of necessary connection. And the necessary connection here was his empathising with the child.

When other philosophers were metaphysically or theoretically occupied, he compared our behaviour and propensities with other members of our animal kingdom. And in so doing lets us know that Darwin's discovery or more properly his grandfather, Erasmus' discovery, was not the sudden discovery it is sometimes depicted. He found it remarkable that all animals in fighting use the same action and avoid harming their companion even though they have no reason to fear his resentment. He gave the example of the lion, tiger and cat using their paws, the ox his horns, the dog his teeth, the horse his heels.

However, even though he had maintained that our deeply rooted beliefs in objects and ourselves and others are the product of the imagination, he would have seen no evidence for imagination in any of the animals to which he had referred. So animals that have no ability to project themselves into the future could have no belief that their fellow adversary would be able to do so, and therefore resentment could only be an issue for beings who can project into the future. And he went on to say that the lack of any real injury they do to each other was evident of the sense they had of the other's pain and pleasure.

But in our observation of such fights, one will just employ sufficient actions to defend themselves from the other, until the heat is dissipated. But Hume could have gone on to ask, being acutely aware of the history of mankind, why the species to which he belonged behaved so differently from the animals. For he would have discovered that man's greater propensity to kill their fellow creatures is due to their ability to visualise, through their imagination, gaining an advantage from the act. The cat or dog or ox has no such ability, and simply employ sufficient energy to preserve their own life. If man could not imagine a possible advantage there would be little or no fatal violence.

Sympathy therefore, and that which Hume referred to many

times in all but name; empathy, are even more important than he had envisaged. When he spoke of there being no quality more remarkable in human action than sympathy, his other phrase; and its consequences, is of as much importance to the topic being discussed here. When he went on to say:

"Accordingly we find that where, besides the general resemblance of our natures, there is any particular similarity in our manners, or character, or country, or language, it facilitates the sympathy."

Furthermore he claimed the stronger the relation between ourselves and someone else, the more easily does the imagination make the transition since we are forming the idea of our own person in the other. And that the humours and turn of thinking of those of the same nation in all probability arose from sympathy, rather than any influence of the soil or climate. It was also his belief that men naturally, without reflection, approve of that character which is most like their own. And in his phrase, without reflection, he is accepting that the degree of empathy one has with one person as opposed to another is entirely involuntary. And following on from his own resolute empiricism he said:

"It has been observed that nothing is ever present to the mind but its perceptions; and that all the actions of seeing, hearing, judging, loving, hating and thinking, fall under this denomination. To approve of one character, to condemn another, are only so many different perceptions."

The outcome of all of this is that we are more capable of empathising with those who are closer to our own nature, character or manners. We are, in other words, more capable of liking those who are most like ourselves. That is of course given that we do like ourselves, and will therefore like those similar to ourselves. So to condemn someone as a racist who does not like someone from another race, as much as someone they can more easily empathise with, is an absurdity   It makes as much sense to condemn someone for being wife-ist, husband-ist, or friend-ist for favouring some individuals against all the others.

So if the qualification for being a racist is someone who likes a significant number of individuals from one racial group more than a significant number of individuals from another racial group, than I am, most certainly a racist. But since empathy is an aspect of the consciousness of every human being, all persons living in a biracial, triracial or multiracial society will also be racist. This is of course, given the understanding that after a pretty finite number of interactions we will have become more disposed to, or less disposed to, another racial group vis a vis our own.

Similarly in a nation of only one racial group there will undoubtedly have arisen either countyists, shireists or cantonists, etcetera. A parent in one locality may well warn their children about the devious, spivishness of people from Nearshire. And in so doing they would be really warning their children about the necessity of being vigilant in their dealings with all persons. Even if in the past, there happened to be the most minute piece of evidence regarding the propensity of persons from Nearshire to be devious, they will be used as somebody onto which to hang the warning. This is simply one of a myriad of defence mechanisms people use as they journey through life. Those defence mechanisms are entirely in keeping with the natural order. They are used by us, as all life forms employ some defence mechanisms. If our evolutionary ancestors had not developed brains and neural pathways enabling their receptors to make almost instantaneous assessments with respect to friend or foe, then we would not have evolved.

The warning mentioned earlier with regard to persons from Nearshire would have been delivered with good humour and also a serious purpose. However, there is no room for humour in the socialist's attitudes to our vital and necessary assessments of others. Their bankrupt ideology has no wise philosophical foundation, so they intercede in an area where they feel votes will be generated for themselves. But their puerile thought processes lead them to believe they occupy a kind of moral high ground, when in reality, they occupy a philosophical quagmire.

We start to make assessments of others when we are weeks, if not days old. Our senses enable us to be aware of the presence of our mothers and we can identify her facial features. We become prejudiced towards our mother. We are biologically programmed to respond favourably to those who benefit us. Equally, we are biologically programmed to respond unfavourably to those who harm us. It is a facet of evolution that dependant young are not indifferent to their care-giver. It is entirely in our interest to show preference to those who are 'good' to us. And should we have difficulty in empathising with a significant number from any racial group we are expected, somehow, to amputate a vital and necessary part of our being to pacify the psyche of the socialist.

I, who live in a multiracial society could delineate a hierarchy of preferences taking into account all racial groups with whom I have had sufficient encounters to enable me to form an opinion. An opinion derived from my degree of empathy. Suffice to say, that at the top of my hierarchy would be the Sikhs.

This is an ethnic group from what was at the time of their origin in the fifteenth century the north west of India, and hold certain beliefs about how life ought to be lived in the here and now. Even though they adhere to a nominally theistic religion it is, I suggest, because their God does not intrude in their core beliefs that makes them such agreeable persons. It was, after all, born out of a belief that factionalism and sectarianism were becoming unacceptably pernicious.

They do not have a professional clergy who in other organised religions invariably abuse their power, and with their laudable concern for the person's life as an individual, they broke the barriers of the caste system. They believe in the great merit of education and in working hard, and working with honesty. They believe they should only live on money that has been honestly earned. They believe they should respect their parents and do no harm to others. They believe in democracy and freedom, and in private enterprise and taking responsibility for their own lives. They believe that respect for others begets love, and love is the core of their ethics. Even though they do not prioritise their beliefs there is one, which is probably most responsible for this ethnic group having the most psychologically healthy men and women; and that is the belief that they should love their children. If a child is loved, cherished and validated, it will grow up to be a loving, psychologically healthy adult.

They believe there are eight virtues a person ought to aspire towards. They are:

Wisdom,	Truthfulness,	Justice,	Temperance,
Patience,	Courage,	Humility,	Contentment.

The presence of the socialist ethic in any society militates against the attainment of all of those. And I shall explain.

The real truth of the socialist's ambition to rid society of differences and inequalities was in order to assist themselves. But this inescapable truth would never be uttered. And even if the passing of certain laws affected other persons, the motivation for their activities was to assist themselves. An obvious truth to any sentient human being is that inequality is essential and unavoidable in every life form – including ours. And to try to eradicate such a feature of life, highlights their paucity of wisdom. Not only should they be cognisant of this; but if one hundred individuals are somehow presented with equal opportunity, one will achieve the greatest success, and another, seeing only the possible catastrophe will do nothing.

So there can be no justice in their interference to take from the most successful to give to the person who has done nothing. There can be no justice in enacting laws which allow for the penalisation of those who have taken responsibility to subsidise those who have abnegated responsibility. There can be no justice in the forceful removal of citizens' money on the pretext of providing a service, which is subsequently denied, when required.

The socialist state encourages intemperance on a grand scale. It gladly funds surgical operations to bring about pathological alterations to prevent over consumption, or to deal with the consequences of over consumption. It stays remorselessly silent on the negative consequences of reliance on carcinogenic mind-altering substances. But gladly funds the purchasing of illicit narcotic replacements from the money taken from those who have never considered the wisdom of relying on such products.

The very essence of socialism is a rejection of the virtue of patience. It promotes the belief that patience and prolonged effort are not the way towards gratification; but the enactment of laws permitting the taking from others most unashamedly is. For any individual under natural law to be able to provide themselves with all of their needs and wants, requires restraint and discipline. But when you promote an ideology that needs to lure people into dependency, it is imperative to maintain a social policy where restraint and discipline are discouraged.

Courage, is a facet of human individuality where extraordinary measures are undertaken for the sake of one's aggrandisement. And courageous acts are nearly always those where the easier option would be to do nothing. But prior to the courageous act the individual will experience the feeling of being starkly alone and yet go on and act courageously. And following that one act the individual will be a stronger character than before. That new strength then enables further acts of courage. And it is acts of courage derived from the acknowledgement of essential aloneness that gives rise to the phenomenon in human life we refer to as; the great or wonderful character. It is not the nation, or the society, or the committee that is courageous; but the individual. And the individual character can never emerge other than from a foundation of truth. But if the truth is twisted by dissemblers and politicians, then, character is submerged by an anodyne ever growing proportion of dependants.

The courageous one takes full responsibility for their own success. They do this having embraced the truth that no one else can be as concerned for their success; as they, themselves. And those who propound the view that other people must take responsibility for the individual are spreading a most pernicious dishonesty. So under socialism courage is not required; others are expected to carry the burden. One individual can initiate a business which grows to be so successful that it becomes the target for socialist scorn; yet one or two decades earlier if the individual concerned was not prepared to be courageous, he may well have been lured into the socialist trap of dependency.

Many writers refer to happiness from time to time. But none, understandably, define it or suggest a formula for its derivation. And all would probably agree, the notion is fairly transitory. However, the notion of contentment is neither transitory nor elusive. All of those who set out in humble circumstances and do not believe that those circumstances are a reflection of their worth as human beings, can achieve contentment. And along the way they can acquire that most priceless feeling that the socialists would deny all. For that feeling is the feeling of a sense of achievement. There can be no more powerful or rewarding or long lasting feeling in human life. But those who are cajoled and lured into dependency can never enjoy that feeling.

The socialists bring about a deprivation far more serious than that which they pretend to attempt to alleviate. And hence we will hear their politicians make the comment year after year, that the gap between those whom they perceive to have too much money, and those they perceive to have too little, is still widening. But when some children grow up in households where there is envy, anger and negativity; and others in households where there is love, contentment and positivity, there can be no other outcome.

So psychologically healthy people are produced because of the ethical beliefs of their parents. And conversely those possessed of a negative ideology will raise offspring which are less healthy psychologically.

So difference exists. And when we encounter that difference, not only do we have a right to form an opinion of another, it would be impossible for us not to form an opinion.

Therefore the cry of racism is essentially a bullying cry. It is made by those who feel they are being wrongly denied something to which they have a right. And furthermore, they are making an accusation against the person doing the denying, that they are evil; because they have made a decision for no reason. Otherwise, if they claim the decision was made for a reason; then they are claiming that the person had no right to make the decision in the first place. The fact that one human being has no right to make a decision with respect to another human being would put us into anthropologically uncharted waters; and would probably necessitate the employment of large numbers of thought police - a thought that seems currently to be not far from the minds of some socialists. But thoughts never arise and actions are never carried out without reason.

If we imagine Britain to be composed of three races; the blue, the green, and the orange race, where Vida belongs to the majority orange race. We must question why learning from experience ought to be outlawed. For more than six months now on boarding her bus, she has decided that if there is no seat

215

available other than that next to a green person she will opt to stand instead. On four occasions in recent years her purse had been stolen while travelling on the bus. And it was only on the last occasion having made the correlation between sitting next to a green person and her purse being stolen, that she has taken this course of action.

In the business she runs, when she looked back over her records she found that she was ten times more likely to encounter punctuality, discipline and productivity problems from blue persons than anyone else. But when she interviews for the next employee she is not allowed to use any of her past experience in arriving at a decision.

However, over the years she has noticed that washing machines made by a certain manufacturer have proved highly unreliable. Her friends also have had similar problems with the same type of machines. However, while she is entitled to choose to buy from a different manufacturer so as to prevent further problems; taking steps to protect her purse, or her business offends the socialist psyche.

In human life where any decision is taken with regard to probabilities, memory is always utilised. No one quite knows how memory functions, but memorable events could be described as the keepsakes of the imagination. If we could not look back and imagine an event it probably could not lodge in memory. And the lodging in memory happens for a purpose. Every single cell in every adult's body is different now than it was seven years ago. And the brain cells that recorded an event ten years earlier have somehow managed to pass on the ability to imagine the event to the new cells. But if this was not important for the survival of homo sapiens then why should it occur?

I suggest that, Vida's memory of past events enable her to protect her interests, and that is why memory exists. Should we, or more importantly, can we short circuit our memory to pacify others? People are different, and we assess all persons according to their behaviour. If every human being treated every other human being as they would wish to be treated themselves then a person's ethnicity would have absolutely no importance. But while state funded organisations exist whose purpose it is to impugn the evil nature of one race vis a vis another, then the message; that respect from all to all, must be shown, will not be heard. Such divisive organisations coupled with religious righteousness do not auger well for harmony.

It does not matter how many times a day a person prays. It does not matter what style they wear their hair or what style of clothing they wear. It does not matter what kind of foods they eat or abstain from eating. It does not matter whether their spiritual leader is descended from a prophet or saint or a meditator. It does not matter whether their God has been to earth or is yet to visit. But what is of paramount importance, is how any believer behaves towards his fellow man. And the behaviour of the Sikhs towards their fellow man, is the true litmus test of the merit of their ethical values. And not until all children are raised in a similarly validated manner will differences between racial groups disappear.

Empathy therefore is that which allows us to receive by communication the inclinations and sentiments of another. And factors such as manners, character, religion, nationality or language, while facilitating empathy with one person, will equally

217

prevent empathy with another, who differs in all such respects. But if I have a religious belief that holds that all those who do not believe as I do, are unclean, it will significantly obstruct my ability to empathise with such non-believers. If I also speak a different language from the non-believers, I may well support a political party that wishes to remove all of the unclean from my country. I would have to prevent my sons and daughters from associating with the children of the unclean. If I also am of a different ethnic origin then the unclean, then there will be a further obstacle to my ability to empathise.

But should I be in a tiny minority in a country of unclean people then I may well try very hard to live in areas amongst my fellow believers. And in so doing I would be indicating that I could not empathise with those I regard as unclean, but I can empathise with my fellow believers. And should I engage in this behaviour it can neither attract approbation or opprobrium. It is simply an indicator of how my empathy is directing my behaviour.

When I was a young boy and my father was telling me that my religion was the one and only true religion, and that those who did not believe were unclean, there was no counsel present to say: "Excuse me sir; but don't you realise what you are saying is a force for sectarianism and disharmony in society?" So it is not possible for me now, to eradicate my former messages. And should I move to live amongst those of a similar belief and ethnic origin as myself, then my actions, according to my earlier definition, would be racist actions. But if there is no law preventing me from indulging in such a racist act, in getting away from my unclean neighbour; then why should my unclean neighbour be obliged to employ me?

When a citizen of Nearshire is involved in an attack on a citizen from another shire it is not reported as a shireist attack. But if the person from the other shire happens to be a member of the blue race, then it is regarded as a racist attack. There seems to be some kind of implication that the first incident was rational criminality, and the second, irrational criminality. The implication being that the first incident had some justification and the second did not.

There is no suggestion in the first case, that the attack was carried out because the Nearshireman did not like the shire origin of the other. But there is every suggestion in the second, that the attack was carried out solely on the basis of the racial origin of the blue person. But if racial origin was sufficient justification for eliciting an attack, by someone from another racial origin, then in Britain, there would be millions of attacks every day. But we know this does not happen. Therefore the distinction made regarding the racial origin of those involved, in reportage of criminality, is an instrument of divisiveness. But just as the divisive belief regarding the different classes suits the socialist purpose; so does their seeing only different races. They don't see a common humanity in the one; or the other.

As already indicated elsewhere, all criminality is derived from the failure of the perpetrator to empathise with their victim. And it will be the duty of an enlightened government and an enlightened people to ensure their children are raised with the minimum number of obstacles to their ability to empathise with their fellow human beings.

11. Flotsam and the Future

Perhaps the best way we can gain an appreciation on where homo sapiens is in the great scheme of things, is to ponder awhile on how long it took one of us to invent the wheel. For the visualisation of this object occurred to someone less than six thousand years ago. And the person who indulged in this visualisation had to have been a da Vinci, Cartwright, or Edison of his day.

Estimates may vary; but certainly for tens of thousands of years, persons like us with the same size brain, and the same latent ability failed to devise this object. And we flatter ourselves if we think that if we were around six thousand years ago we would have invented this device. But currently when we are surrounded by technological innovation we can easily delude ourselves about our greatness. For however impressive the new technologies may be, they have been just one tiny advance after tiny advance on Shockley's transistor of 1948. And that in its turn an advance on its more crude forerunner. But tiny advances is all we have made, even though, because of the retention and dissemination of information, those advances are now happening more frequently.

But we make a grave mistake if we lose sight of who we are, and what we are. For an accurate measure of our intelligence we must ask ourselves how many people on this planet today would have invented the wheel six thousand years ago? Would they have been innovative then, when they are not innovative now? The truth is that we in our turn are only a tiny advance on our primate cousins. The facility we have because of our larger brains is that of imagination. Some people may prefer to speak of our greater intelligence. But that intelligence which distinguishes us from other primates is provided to us from our versatile imagination. And the degree to which one person may appear to be more intelligent or less intelligent than another is dependent on the versatility or agility of their imagination.

For if we consider what we are capable of doing; some people make great play on our ability to reason. But reason, is only; calculation, foresight, or planning. And in the non-rational area we; hope, and have concern for the future and recollect the past. So all our thought processes are imagination dependent.

Imagination is that which sets us apart and determines who we are. And what is most crucial of all to understand is that simply because we have one extra facility, we are not set apart from nature. There are those who believe we are somehow a special life form. There are those who believe that we are somehow unique. There are those who believe that objects in space six trillion miles away, just one light year, are there for our sake. And there are those who believe that objects in space hundreds of light years away, were created by a supernatural being who looks like us. And some of those people are leaders of nations; such as in Britain.

But it has not just been in the political arena where the misplacement of mankind has led to error. Many learned persons addressing areas of concern, have employed stylised stilted notions of what we are; and have therefore provided little of value. One of those areas of concern is that of criminology.

It is natural that we ought to have a concern as to why some individual human beings offend against others. Since if we could understand more about the compulsion or inclination to offend, we may be able to bring about a reduction in such instances. And that would seem like a reasonable aspiration. But the persons involved in investigating the matter have decided to look to an area that can provide no real assistance to them. And that is, to the environment. Maybe some of those criminologists choose to look to the environment for political reasons and others later, not knowing what else to do, just followed the earlier path. And it would have suited the socialist agenda to blame the environment for rising crime; since they could then set about spending enormous sums to change the environment.

But whether they were politically motivated or just vainly searching in the dark, no impact has been made on that force which generates the law breaker. For it was impossible for them to gain insight while vilifying the inanimate environment. However, if they had concentrated on the personal environment alone they may have happened upon some wisdom. For the forces that create a criminal, are the interactions that person has had with others, and the environment plays no part whatever. Because the simple truth; which ought to have been readily available to anyone who wanted to see, is that a criminal is created because of the manner in which he is raised and nothing to do with where he is raised. And if they were so persuaded by the environment argument, ought they not to have asked very serious questions about the escapees; those who grew up in precisely the same environment and did not embark on a life of crime as some of their contemporaries.

But this would have led to some uncomfortable answers. For the only difference between the two is the quality of parenting. And if emphasis were to be placed on the quality of parenting then the revealing spotlight would come to rest on behaviour. And if behaviour started to be examined it would call the entire ethos of socialism into question.

So we can see why the inanimate environment became the very convenient target. Very convenient, because extra expenditure on any cause, however unjustified, is a vote buying cause. An examination of behaviour would inevitably draw in the issue of personal responsibility. And if such a situation arose it would be the political equivalent of the identity parade; it would leave the individual. But we know that the socialist ideology only sees 'the rich' and 'the poor', and hence no exercise was entered into, which would have removed that time honoured tenet of socialism.

Disciplined parents raise disciplined children. Disciplined children do not go on to commit crime. Everything a child sees, hears and experiences, before he is five years of age determines whether or not he goes on to offend against others. And if he does go on to offend against others, two people, no more, no less, are responsible for his behaviour. And his offending against others will be the consequence of his parents offending against him. The offending is simply displaced. And the essence of that offending, was in their failure to empathise with his needs at important times in his young life.

Should he go on to commit violent offences against others, he is only retaliating against the physical assaults on him. The

223

empathy void in his psychological profile does not allow him to identify mentally with his victim. He proceeds to assault others in an effort to perform some kind of reconciliation with his void. He does not see that it is wrong; for those who provided him with shelter and food when he was four, believed it was right. And he took on their belief with no facility to question it. If we want the proof of this quest to fill the empathy void we only have to observe the phenomenon of football hooliganism.

This is just one of the many areas of crime that have escalated since the socialist interference in society. And the people engaged in this activity will spend large sums of money in the effort to placate their void. They travel to different cities and sometimes to different countries to confront like-minded damaged people, in a quest to enjoy the fight. And the like minded people wherever they find them, will be the children of the beneficiaries of socialism. It has come to mean that association football sporting occasions require police planning befitting a military exercise.

But if a young boy of three or four sat and watched his father repair a chair on a Saturday afternoon, how different things would be. If his father explained what he was doing and why he was doing it, and allowed his son to help, then something of real value would be happening. He would be demonstrating that he valued his son; he would be setting an example for his son; and he would be demonstrating that he valued property. And his son would not be able at a later stage, to tear up seating in a football stadium and use it as a weapon against the police. But when a hooligan grows up in property that belongs to someone else, and when a broken piece of furniture is replaced by new furniture, bought from the social security budget; then there is no respect for property. And those who are capable of throwing other people's property at the police will have known no discipline.

For even if the police did not act as the enforcers of law and order; the very fact that they wear uniforms intonates discipline; and as such, they attract the wrath of the undisciplined hooligan. And when some well meaning criminologists made the correlation between environment and crime, they omitted the vital aspect of discipline. Of course there is a connection between indiscipline and crime, and of course there is an observed connection between crime and environment, but simply because; the same kind of individual with the same level of indiscipline will live in similar circumstances.

Undisciplined people are poor at managing their lives. They are poor at performing the necessary functions to retain employment. They are poor at obeying laws. They are poor at conducting themselves in such a manner that would make other people kindly disposed to them. They are poor at making the connection between dissipate behaviour and undesirable consequence. And when all those areas of poverty lead to a person living in circumstances that the socialist politicians regard as unacceptable, they take money from disciplined citizens and redirect it in their favour.

Before the socialist ideology permitted the interference in such a manner, people did live in poor circumstances. But they lived in poor circumstances because of their poor attitudes and poor behaviour. And outside interference instead of facilitating improvement obstructs improvement.

Long before the invention of the wheel societies had

progressed; and that progression lasted up until the end of the nineteenth century. And progression to that point gives us far more things to be impressed with than anything that has happened under socialist regimes. And in every era during that progression, there have been poor individuals, and in every era, individuals were free to set about improving their lives if they so wished. And that progression led from the poor, to the not so poor, to the well off. That progression is a natural progression, and anyone who believes in the forceful intervention in a natural sequence, is philosophically illiterate.

For there is no obliteration of the truth that; that which is obtained too cheaply is esteemed too lightly. In all of human life there are interdependent bonds which remain constantly taut in every area, unless there is interference by a third party. If I pass a shop window and see an item I might like to have, which costs five thousand pounds; I have several choices. I can go ahead and buy it if I think the price is reasonable. I can refuse to buy it if I think the price is too much. I can try to negotiate with the vendor to sell it more cheaply; or I can travel to another part of town, where costs are lower, and try to buy more cheaply there. If I buy; the bond remains taut between myself and the vendor. If I refuse to buy, the bond also remains taut, because of my degree of demand against the vendor's preparedness to supply at the given price. If I negotiate down to a price that I am prepared to pay, at which the vendor is prepared to sell, then the bond also remains taut. If I travel to another part of town to obtain the product more cheaply still, it will be because of my available money against the lower overheads of a different vendor and the bond still remains taut.

However, if a third party intervenes and pays all the

overheads of the vendor because they believe he needs a subsidy; or pays money to me because they believe I am underprivileged, they cause a distortion in the bond. The bond is either going to become over distended, or slack, and one or other of the parties is going to suffer in the short term; and both in the long term. And when a third party intervenes between two parties such as in the state's attempt to supply services; then there is much more serious contortion and unravelling, when all the bonds between the two parties are completely severed. So for something to be esteemed appropriately it has to be acquired under the circumstance of that bond remaining taut. And when there is overwhelming interference with those bonds, there results a distorted society.

I now wish to qualify my earlier phrase regarding dissipate behaviour and undesirable consequence. The undesirable consequence may well be the assessment of an outsider paying excessive taxes; and it is a value judgement of his. But rarely if ever, does the individual engaged in dissipate behaviour, regard the consequences of their actions as undesirable. For if they did; the behaviour would not continue. But we know such behaviour continues decade after decade. Because what is really in play, is self-destructive behaviour. A wise man once said;

"nobody can be poor for very long, unless they are quite comfortable with the idea."

And nobody can be regarded as poor in Britain, unless they are engaged in self-destructive behaviour. It would take nobody any more than five years to get away from difficult circumstances unless low self esteem determined that they were comfortable with their circumstances. But low self-esteem is the result of being raised by parents who had no love to give, let alone the provision of unconditional love. And then there results the vicious cycle, something that has existed in all eras; but under socialist ideology those vicious cycles have been multiplied many fold.

***

A leading socialist suggested recently that the issue of domestic violence was a fitting area for his involvement. But if ever there was an area of human life that was not fitting for someone completely lacking in an understanding of human nature, this has to be it. For if a man needs to be in a relationship with a woman who assaults him on a regular basis, then he will go out of his way to find such a person. And if a woman needs to be in a relationship with a man who assaults her on a regular basis, then she will go out of her way to find him. And should the socialist be awarded more taxes to employ more civil servants to bring about some kind of separation of the two people, then in their next relationship they will find a person with a similar profile, but just with a different name. For people get into relationships with the kind of person they need at that time in their lives.

The woman, when she was a young girl needed physical contact from her father. But he was incapable of giving affectionate physical contact. Instead, he was very capable of being physically abusive to her. And she unconsciously created situations that provided him with an excuse to be physically abusive. She felt that any physical contact from her father was better than no contact. It gave her the sense of security she wanted. Similarly the man, when a young boy, created circumstances to rouse his mother to anger, so she would assault

228

him, giving him the only physical contact he had.

Now both people search in their own way for grown-ups who will take the place of their abusive parents, to give them the security they crave in adult life. And even though they may appear to be in adult life, they are simply grown up children. For such a degree of abuse, and such a degree of empathy loss arrests the normal development of the individual and transition from childhood to adulthood will not take place. Even the most skilled team of psychoanalysts would not be able to effect that which would be the only thing of value. That being; the retrospective provision of empathy. And of course that is impossible. The two individuals who accepted a kind of poisoned empathy will have to seek out life partners with the same degree of psychological damage as their abusive parents.

But it is not only in cases such as the above where childhood experiences govern the pair-bonding dynamic. All cases of pair bonding are determined by the psychological profile of the two persons. And the process can be expressed, which in no way tries to reduce the complexity of the matter, in numerical terms. Let us take it, that for pair bonding to occur and have a significant duration the coming together or addition of the two numbers must total one 'hundred'. When two people have been raised by loving parents and are psychologically healthy they will be numbered at 'fifty' each, and their pair bond will total one hundred. Whereas if someone is psychologically damaged to the extent that they number 'thirty seven', they will have to seek out someone whose profile numbers 'sixty three'. Similarly if someone is damaged to such a degree that they number 'ninety seven' they will have to seek out someone who is damaged to such a degree that they number 'three'. And should anyone believe that someone who is numbered 'three' would ever be happy with a 'fifty', they are deluding themselves.

The damaged person must seek out those who compensate in some way for their empathy loss. But unfortunately it is never compensation. The damaged person will seek out an individual similar to the parent who was responsible for the empathy loss. They are in effect giving their parent a second chance. They are saying – why can't you see that I'm not a bad person? But there will be no seeing; because the partner has been chosen deliberately because they can't see, just like the original parent couldn't see.

So when a socialist politician believes he can provide a solution to an instance of domestic violence he is merely betraying his lack of understanding of the delicate nature of human relationships. His action would be similar to someone seeing a small weed in the centre of a large flower garden and sending in a large excavating machine to uproot it. It could take it up, along with a huge amount of soil and numerous flowers. The only enlightened response would be to wait for the frosts of time to kill the weed. But an enlightened response is that which we shall never get from those busy looking for problems on which to spend tax payers' money.

So understanding the psychology of the individual or understanding the closest of personal relationships, will never get in the way of those wishing to impugn the environment. And criminologists in assessing the habitual burglar will not look to the quality of his parenting. For what can be certain is that he witnessed no respect for property in his early years. He is able to break into many houses because he cannot empathise with those who own them. He cannot empathise with those who disciplined themselves for many years and made many sacrifices to buy property, and furnished it with belongings of their choice. He has no compunction in making off with their belongings since he does not have to go beyond his empathic domain. He may have heard his parents describe those living in better circumstances than themselves as snobs, and hence he regards them as fair game.

And should he leave burglary and turn his hand to stealing expensive cars and crashing them, it will also be because he cannot empathise with the owners. In every area of crime whether it be against property or the person it is only possible due to a failure of the perpetrator to empathise with his victim.

And sooner or later after the due process of cautions, conditional discharges and suspended sentences, he will have to spend some time in prison. The reason for the court's decision was that it felt the public needed to be protected from his further offending. The prison wardens now have the task of imposing some kind of discipline on someone to whom it has been practically unknown. And one would imagine that someone who has eventually been sent to prison for the sake of the protection of the public, would not have much power. But we would be wrong.

Because just as bullying is promoted under the social policy, and in all likelihood the parents of the prisoner will have been allowed to bully others to make them pay for all of their needs; bullying is a part of the penal system. The penal system has empowered the prisoner and concomitantly disempowered the public. The penal system has capitulated to the unspoken threat of further criminal behaviour by the prisoner, and tells him that if he would only refrain, he would only need to serve half his sentence. So the bully wins. And the justification for such a policy is that the prison system could not possibly contain all of those serving full sentences, and, accommodate all those being newly sentenced. So the safety valve to release the stench from the results of socialist policies is introduced. For socialist policies generate more and more people who behave irresponsibly, and criminal behaviour is only irresponsible behaviour of an extreme form.

But we must have the utmost sympathy for prisoners. For their parents started to put them in prison when they were two, three, four and five years of age. Without socialism their parents would have had to wait until they had the necessary resources to bring children into the world. They would have been wiser, more responsible and more disciplined; but instead they readily accepted the fraudulently proffered socialist sop. With the result being; an overcrowded prison system, despite the capitulation to bullying. And some people are often surprised at the extent of recidivism. They make the point that if someone is once sentenced for a crime they would not wish to re-offend and return to prison. They make the facile comment that they must somehow like it in prison. But the understanding of the life long pattern of offending is in the understanding of the life long existence of the empathy void. Just as the empathy void will never allow them to empathise with others, and dictates their re-offending, so too a significant number will not be able to manage their lives outside prison. They did not see their parents successfully managing their lives. And now they too become dependants on the state; within the realms of the penal system.

Then there are those who are of such an age that they cannot be charged with any offence regardless of how many they have committed. Those are normally young boys who are out of control. The sons of two parents, or far more often one parent, who are out of control themselves. And in the vain attempt to deal with such cases we can witness the true extent of the shameful abuse of the taxpayer. One meeting alone surrounding one case will involve youth offending specialists, doctors, education welfare officers, police and the inevitable social worker. And at the end of their meeting, if not one person had suggested the abandonment of the corrupt social policy; which gave rise to this boy's behaviour, then their time will have been entirely wasted. Even if they were miraculously capable of regressing this boy; and have him raised by adults who were mature enough to provide him with adequate love and attention, it would only resolve one case. And the civil servants can rest assured that there are thousands of others being generated by the socialist ideology, ensuring their future salaries are guaranteed.

And if we wanted proof that those who do not understand the causes of problems, will make them considerably worse; we only need to recall recent statements. A socialist politician suggested that the state should fund child-minders for the babies of single mothers so as to enable them to work. And this had followed a statement some days earlier when she had spoken of "the intractable problem of rising crime". But she will never understand that those young females had snatched the role of motherhood, as soon as possible to ensure they avoided the adult world of work in the first place. And it is because of all the inducements that are in place, which encourage that; and other kinds of irresponsible behaviour, which has led to the increase in crime.

So for criminologists who talk about the environment, and

for non socialist politicians who may be interventionists, they ought to consider this fact. Circumstances do not determine the life of an individual; they reveal the kind of life the individual is leading.

***

Some people have made the extraordinary suggestion that socialism and Christianity have much in common. And in one sense they may have. But only in the sense of the common duplicity of the politicians of the one, and the clergy of the other. We can readily ignore the many instances where clerics do not practise what they preach. But during very serious street criminality in Britain a leading cleric suggested the reason for the rioting was; poor housing. And whilst we don't have to dwell on the illogic of such a statement, we can observe subsequent actions. The religious organisation of which this man was a representative, had billions of pounds of investments at the time, and every penny remained in tact.

Not even enough money was removed to build just one house, to prevent one family in the future going out and destroying other people's property. And all of their money remained invested because they are consumed by the same hypocrisy as the socialists. The socialists who extol the virtues of one type of education, but send their own children elsewhere. The socialists who stress the importance of the environment and carelessly pollute it themselves. The socialists who support increases in welfare payments, but keep their own money in offshore trusts, to avoid contributing towards the increases. And when we consider the one and only precious precept of Christianity – do unto others as you would have others do unto

234

you – we can assess how closely it comes to socialism in action.

Right from the outset socialism has been driven by enmity of others. It has been a tearing down rather than a building up ideology. Had it not been for the engine of the trade union movement it would probably have faded out of existence. And trade unionism is about getting advantages, at the expense of others, by the use of force. I don't recall enmity, destruction and the use of force, being part of Christianity. But when people band together for the purposes of blackmail, and treat the employer as the enemy, is he not their neighbour? And should they not love their neighbour? And did the workers at the numerous failed nationalised industries care about the neighbours who were supplying the taxes for their wages and salaries? And did the workers at British Leyland who were manifestly more interested in taking strike action than building acceptable more vehicles, care about the damage to the British economy? When they were not just causing immense damage at home, but ensuring billions flowed out into French, Italian, German and Japanese bank accounts; who were producing acceptable motor vehicles.

And if I should not like to be forced to pay ninety eight percent income tax, who should I ensure it is done unto others? And if I should not like, as the owner of a property to have less rights than a tenant, why should I ensure it is done unto others? And if I should not like to be caused immense hardship because of the subsequent absence of rentable accommodation, why should I ensure it was done unto others? And if I would not wish to be trapped into dependency, why should I ensure it is done unto others? But we know that the purpose of their heinous Rent Acts, were to force people into their clutches, where they could be controlled and manipulated for ever more.

It has already been stated that the Christian ethic seems to produce more acceptable societies in which to live than any other theistic belief. Therefore it has been a good force in many societies. But in how many societies has socialism been a good force? Socialism has caused economic destruction everywhere it has been tried, including Britain. And it does this because it is a negation of the life force. It destroys initiative, enterprise and morale. It draws people into a mind set of self pity and blaming others. And since there will always be some who are wiser, more industrious, more disciplined, and therefore living more comfortable lives, they can become the targets of the socialists.

They can tell their supporters that they ought to feel sorry for themselves, that if other people didn't have so much, they would have more. They spread their negativity widely. They tell their audience that they are not trusted to conduct their own lives successfully. They are told that they don't have the wherewithal to function as free citizens. They are told they don't have the intelligence to spend their own money wisely. They are told that if they would only hand over their money to the socialists they would provide them with truly wonderful services.

And then when a great chasm exists between earlier promises and delivered reality; they ask for more money. Then they have to accept, that the objects of their enmity were not as numerous as their earlier rhetoric suggested, and the levelling process did not produce as much revenue as expected. So an ideology that brings about social and economic destruction can hardly have much to do with; do unto others as you would have others do unto you.

But no matter how great the clarity of the earlier failure; since they don't understand the reason for that failure, they will go on to bring about further failure. And one of those areas of failure is now in the industry of dependency creation. This arises from the belief that the government must intervene on behalf of the individual. But where is the legitimacy of this intervention? In every society under natural law there will always be those who are furthest back, and those who are furthest forward. As a life form that has evolved, no other circumstance could ever exist. But the intervention tries to effect a moving forward of those at the back by hampering the progress of those at the front. And this intervention obstructs the natural flow of life.

Those who have made unwise decisions or acted unwisely are prevented from learning, growing or becoming stronger people. They are bailed out; and will continue to make unwise decisions. The intervention is analogous to the unenlightened parent who will not remove the stabilisers from his son's bicycle. He is afraid his son may fall over and cut his knees. But falling over and cutting our knees is an essential part of growing up. We must endure the pain in order to learn how to run or cycle properly. But the intervention prevents the experience of pain by using other people's money as the stabiliser, and hence no learning occurs. And when parents go through life attached to the socialist stabilisers, their children will be less well able to deal with the prospect of falling over, and will become, metaphorically speaking, the agoraphobics of tomorrow.

But then if the second-generation victims of intervention require a handful of medical and welfare attendants, it is wonderfully supporting the socialist cause. One socialist in particular reiterates ad nauseam his desire to fund the raising of other people's babies and young children. The message is driven home time after time, that it is not the parents' responsibility; it is his. Not only is his intervention in this area accepting that there is an irresponsible society already; but it is encouraging its growth still further.

When an individual has brought about their own penury it is nobody else's business; unless some other individual or individuals voluntarily make it their business. Voluntary intervention is perfectly in keeping with the natural order. But the state's intervention, is forced intervention, and as such is totally illegitimate. The socialist can only intervene using other people's money that has been forcefully removed from them. One has to ask about the legitimacy of forcing people to pay money to others to whom they would not voluntarily pay money. For if they would voluntarily pay money to others; then there was never any need for the socialist ideology in the first place. And since it is in existence it must use force. But when we remember that the socialists are governed by self-interest; the motivational mystery is resolved, when we observe the electoral gratitude expressed as a result of their generosity with other people's money. A gratitude that allows them to continue to exorcise their jealousy and greed, and adversely affect their enemies; those who do take responsibility for their own lives; and the lives of their children.

Prior to socialism, if any individual was living in penury, everyone else in the neighbourhood was well aware of the fact. And if assistance was provided it was voluntarily provided. And in that provision there was healthy mutually beneficial human interaction. There was opportunity for conviviality and friendship. There was opportunity for advice, encouragement and sympathy. And the existence of this aspect of human life, driven by empathy, is as authentic and natural as our facility to feel pain when we fall and cut our knees.

But the greatest diversity exists between voluntary intervention and forced intervention. And that is in the ability of the individual to monitor precisely the effects of their assistance. If they see that their intervention is doing more harm than good they immediately modify their behaviour and withhold all assistance. And this in its turn, is as authentic as their earlier attempts to assist. No individual would continue with assistance on observing it to be counter-productive. And again they are governed by their own empathy. They feel that if they had been in such a predicament, and had received such assistance, they would have improved their circumstances. And seeing no improvement, they put a 'stop loss order' on their intervention. They know that human behaviour and response to others, ought to be the guiding principle in determining their further involvement.

But the state has no eyes, no ears, no consciousness, no feeling, no empathy, and no monitoring ability. And it continues its overwhelming intervention in citizen's personal lives, despite it being so obviously counter-productive. The State eradicated much of the authentic voluntary assistance that did exist. And they did this in order to gain control. After all, those involved in the voluntary assistance of others cannot be manipulated at election time. But those who are paid within the system of forced intervention can be manipulated. Whilst not one individual would fund a single bottomless pit of apparent worthiness; the State funds millions of bottomless pits. And while this gives great satisfaction to the socialists, the inauthentic nature of their intervention ought to be recognised.

Under voluntary intervention there is humanity, concern, and genuine regard for others. But under the State's forced intervention, what was earlier regarded as a kindness, is now, a right. And therein lies the great truth distortion. For in order for there ever to be a right to anything, there must be an obligation on another to provide it. And who chooses the citizens in any society, who have the duty to provide that to which others have a right?

Sadly in socialist democracies, those citizens who shoulder the highest degree of responsibility for themselves and their own families, are the ones forced to shoulder the responsibility for those citizens who show no such inclination in their own regard. And those who believe in the maintenance of such a situation, are those who believe that nature must be coerced. The addictive personalities must never be allowed to suffer the disadvantages of their own addiction. They must be brought in to enjoy the new addiction. The addiction to other people's forced assistance; whereas in the past, under individual discretional intervention, such addictive personalities would be forced into some kind of self-confrontation. But now; no such self-confrontation is ever necessary.

Long before psychology became a science, experimental or otherwise, Joseph Butler in 1740 had written on the importance of childhood events and how those determined the character and station in life, of the individual. He spoke of the importance of enlightened self-love and how it is necessary for; friendship, compassion, and parental love. He saw that true benevolence could only result from enlightened self-love. And he wrote the following:

"The law of life is not to save us trouble but to impose it, and enable us to go through it. What we become seems ever dependent upon what we do. And everywhere we are to choose improvement at the price of effort, or misery as the result of neglect."

Those few words were as true then, as they are now, as they will be in a thousand years. He saw that virtue was in following nature rather than trying to oppose her. But what we have with socialist interference is the prevention of citizens having to confront their troubles. There is no becoming, because there is no doing; there is just reliance on others.

At the moment of the interference, the individual becomes stuck, and remains stuck. It is necessary to engage in effort to bring about improvement, and should we neglect to do so we bring about misery. And it is not that numerous individuals in a socialist state neglect to engage in their own improvement, they are actively and deliberately encouraged not to do so. Should they bring about their own improvement they might escape dependency and not be ripe for manipulation at election time.

And what is certain is that parents who understood the importance of self-love could never raise the child who would become the addictive personality. Parents who love themselves will raise the child who loves himself. And the person who loves himself will have no need for any substance to assist in dealing with; or in blocking out reality. People who block out reality are blocking out themselves; because they don't like themselves. Those who love themselves are perfectly comfortable with reality and have no need to block it out. And we can be afforded the clearest evidence as to how much people love themselves, by how they treat their physical bodies. Then when we observe the changing health status of millions of Britons because of the way they treat their physical bodies, we can be certain that they were not raised by loving parents.

The family unit is not a political unit. Before politics the family unit existed. The family unit is a natural unit. The male and the female of our species have always participated in the raising of their offspring. But the socialist ideology has done its utmost to break up this unit. There may well have been votes to be gained because of their activity; but how enormously costly to society those votes have been. As soon as the facility and encouragement is in place to allow units to break up, or to obviate the need for any unit at all, there will inevitably be an exponential increase, generation after generation of those lacking in self love. For no individual can give, that which they do not have.

Then Butler was just an enlightened English philosopher who understood the importance of self-love and the love of others. Britain in its governance would do well to take note of this man's philosophy. But instead; we are governed by an ideology much more in keeping with the thinking of a criminal on the run from Prussia, who was consumed with hatred. And this ought to be a reminder and an indicator as to where homo sapiens is in our level of intelligence.

For when mankind makes a mistake, that mistake tends to remain for centuries. And the mechanism that holds the mistake in place is that of; assumption. People assume that because a particular circumstance exists it must be right or good. But it takes unreasonable, obstinate, nonconformist type of people to bring about improvement. Just like the inventor of the wheel or transistor or any other invention had to be derived from the mind of unreasonable kind of people. Others may well have felt like saying; why do you want to change things; why can't you be happy the way things are?

But it is one thing to be missing an artefact that would improve the quality of our lives; it is quite another to be living under an ideology which is carrying out an injustice, in an unnatural drive towards equality. Especially when the policy adhered to in that drive, is unleashing forces for social degeneration.

Hence until sufficient time has elapsed for unreasonable people to dwell on the consequences, we will have to contend with the status quo. And we have the evidence that insufficient time has elapsed. Since it must have been so mortifying for the socialists to loose control of their failed nationalised industries, they vowed vengeance on their return to power. And they have taken their vengeance in the creation of a new nationalised industry. And that is the industry of red tape and regulation. Because just as they need their supporters to be addicted to dependence, they themselves are addicted to control. They are not capable of seeing that it was government intervention that brought about the failure of their beloved industries because of the breaking of the bond between customer and service provider. But now, they want to intrude in all businesses large and small and strangle them with regulation.

They are simply not capable of empathising with business people; who are positive, enterprising, optimistic kind of people. While they themselves are negative, suspicious, controlling kind of people. It is instructive to note, that one of the few people in business to have been clearly identified with the socialists, saw fit to steal his own employee's pension funds. So success is rarely associated with negative people. And success in government is never associated with socialist parties. Business people are prepared to take risks, and if they do not achieve all they want the first time they learn from the experience and try again. This requires a positive attitude. It requires a belief in self. It requires the belief that they can be the masters of their own destiny. And because their belief is so at odds with socialist ideology, they must be brought under bureaucratic, stifling, stultifying, cynical control. A control which squeezes the very life blood from a healthy vibrant economy.

Vast numbers of civil servants will sit in offices shuffling form after form, taking many months over maters that could be processed in minutes; if the dynamic of the market had any bearing on the subject. And they will have no concern for the costs incurred while the business person waits for the due process of job creation to be celebrated in some government department. After all, it is not their money. As for the socialists they will be happy because their enemies; the positive, independent people are being obstructed, impoverished and frustrated.

Perhaps the expectation is that if sufficient private businesses are forced to give up the unequal struggle, then the state can step in, justified in the delusion that other people have a duty to provide jobs for other people. Such activity would be akin to breaking a man's leg and then offering him a walking stick. But whatever damage may have been done in the past, they still believe they have a right and an obligation to intervene in the market place.

However, there can be little doubt that if all unnecessary

state tentacles were withdrawn there could only be beneficial results. And some of those tentacles are in the area of discrimination and employment protection law. When the State can only legitimately exist for the common good; those laws, were brought into existence for the particular 'good'.

And when such a situation arises it means that one citizen is forced to endure some loss so that another citizen can enjoy some gain. And it has to be asked under natural law what right some people have to enact such legislation that brings about such distortion. What it means in practice is that some employers are forced to retain some employees because of the prohibitive legal costs that can follow any dismissal. And therefore they have to pay more money each month than the person is actually worth. Meaning that some employees have to compensate for the inadequacy of another.

Even though there may be a period when an employee does not have so much protection, many ensure they wait until that period has elapsed before becoming relaxed about their inadequacy. And while such situations exist, the morale of the competent employees is adversely affected. Because of the nature of the market place, no employer would ever wish to lose the services of a competent employee. Therefore, such an individual has no need of some artificial mechanism to ensure he remains in employment. Hence the effect of employment legislation is to ensure some people who are adversely affecting a business remain in their positions.

Similarly employers are under pressure to employ individuals from what politicians conveniently refer to as minority groups. But if an individual does not present himself as the best candidate for a particular job, there ought to be no compulsion that they be employed, regardless of what minority group they can be regarded as emanating from. And should they be employed, it constitutes positive discrimination. But if there is positive discrimination then that act entails discrimination against someone else.

So there can be no basis under any system of justice for some people to instruct others as to how they should run their business. Any employer ought to have the freedom to employ whom he likes, for whatever reason he likes, for as long as he likes. The only possible legitimate activity that could be engaged in by any politician who claims to have concern for another's prospects of employment; is to establish their own business and employ only those whom they feel are being somehow disadvantaged. And they in their turn ought to have complete freedom to employ only those from one minority group if they so wished. And if the business, while in competition with others, remained a viable entity he would be demonstrating that others had made unwise decisions. But unfortunately we never have the opportunity to observe such a spectacle. Because socialists who intervene in the market place are far more generous with other people's money than they are with their own. Their only motivation for the interference was in the belief that employers; far from being essential facets of a health economy, were engaged in wrong doing, in employing those whom they considered to be most suitable for their business.

And while such a situation exists some aspect of free enterprise is lost. When the state intervenes on behalf of the individual, it is the case, without exception, that an actual wrong is introduced in an attempt to eradicate an imagined wrong. For the imagined wrong is that inequality is wrong. But inequality is neither right nor wrong, it is simply an inescapable aspect of nature. If some person does not have a job it may be because of, for example, their hostile, aggressive attitude. Then that particular person is on their own unique path in life.

Under natural law they would have to bring such behaviour under control, and employ greater civility to gain employment. They would be shaped, by having to learn, to satisfy their own needs. And having done so, they would have made progress along their path. But when the state intervenes to ensure such a person remains in employment, or gains employment, instead of someone else, then they obstruct progress. The intervention is often entered into because of the numbers of complainers and blamers. Those people who do not have all that they want and complain about other people's unfairness or blame them for doing them down in some way. Such people want that which will never bring them satisfaction. They want other people to improve their lives. And we do notice how such people are so extraordinarily likely to support socialism.

So anti-discrimination law actually engenders discrimination. And employment law, although not having the power to create one job; does ensure artificially sustained positions, which are not an insignificant aspect of general productivity being at thirty percent. So what can be said is that when the state intervenes to try to effect some supposed good in the particular case, the consequences are consistently counter-productive.

***

Over time, philosophers have engaged themselves with speculative relationships in areas such as resemblance, identity, contrariety, and space and time. And all of their energies were solely directed towards the acquisition of knowledge, truth or belief. At least it is reasonable to suppose that there was such an aspiration governing their preoccupations. But many seem to have been content, that concern alone with such matters, was deserving of approbation.

However, truth is much more readily accessible than via concerns over contiguity and distance; the existence or otherwise of space; the derivation of our idea of space; or whether motion is necessarily attendant on both time and space. Such matters are not a consideration for the commonality of mankind. And when such philosophers moved away from their desks and lived in the real world, neither were they for them. So philosophical questions that do not have a bearing on our lives are hardly worthy of consideration.

But matters of space and time pertinent to our daily lives, are, having a bearing on Vida's quality of life as she waits at her bus stop. A destination she arrived at twenty minutes ago having walked the short distance from her workplace. And she possibly expected that the space between herself and her bus was lessening all the while. But it was not. The bus that she ought to have been able to board is stationary at the depot. Meanwhile the glass screening of the shelter that could have given some protection from the swirling rain is lying in numerous tiny fragments on the ground. Seven other people have joined the queue since she arrived. Earlier in the day a controller took a telephone call regarding the illness of one of the drivers. A long way in the distance she can pick out a red object that might be the numbered bus she wants. The previous night and early morning there was a very interesting cricket match being beamed into British homes from Australia. As the bus gets closer there appears to be a solid mass of bodies inside. The driver was very interested in cricket and continued to watch until the final ball. She manages to squeeze onto the crowded bus with two others as luckily three passengers disembarked at the same stop. His wife had called to tell his employer that he was ill since he was simply too tired to get up. She had spent thirty five minutes waiting in the wind and rain for the bus. The driver will not go to work until the following week. He will be paid for his time at home just as if he had spent his time providing a service for passengers.

So time spent waiting, or time paid for, or space between modes of transport and ourselves are relevant in so far as they impact on human life. While she stood shivering in the rain she was being told many things by the operators of the transport system.

"Your time is not important. We don't care how long you have to wait. The service we operate is for our benefit. We don't see you as a customer. You are just someone who boards our buses, pays us some money and gets off elsewhere. Customers can take their money elsewhere, but you have to wait at the same stop every day. We are not going to lose any money no matter how dissatisfied you are. Even if you hire a taxi we will still get your taxes through our subsidy. If you feel like making a complaint about the service, you can go ahead and try, but it wont get you very far. We have all the power; you have none."

And of course they would be right about having all the power. When any service is being offered and there is no direct

249

relationship between the customers and the self-interest of the service providers, then the resulting service will be abysmal. Power is with the management of the system; since the government has guaranteed to compensate for any failure with further subsidy. The fulfilling of the concept that a transportation service for citizens ought to be in place, seems to be sufficient to keep governments content. The fact that individuals have to endure delays, overcrowding and inoperational equipment is of no consequence, as long as the concept is being fulfilled. The management, as in all State funded services, are secure in the knowledge that whatever their level of performance, it will have no bearing on their remaining in employment.

Some years earlier a newly appointed over officious manager decided on a course of action regarding the level of absenteeism due to supposed ill health. He was prepared to adhere to the normal terms of the disciplinary procedures. However, when a senior manager informed him of the likely outcome he was forced to become rather less officious. Such attempts were made in the past, but were met with the threat of strike action by the unions. They regarded any such activity by the management as victimisation of their brothers; and if any action were taken, they would remain on strike until any serial absenteeist was reinstated.

Naturally when management are not in competition with anyone else, and do not stand to lose in any way from such capitulation, they do not see the point in upsetting the apple-cart. But Vida's power is sacrificed by a comfortably isolated management on the altar of union power. When she cannot band together with all other passengers and acquire the power to adversely affect the wages and salaries of all those involved in her invalidation, then she has no power. All service requirement and service provision operates on the basis of self-interest. And when that is removed from the equation, at least one party will be made to suffer.

The acceptance by the state that some people in the provision of public services can band together, acquire and use power against those citizens funding their wages and salaries is a perverse arrangement. It is a perversion of justice. For there is no escaping the fact that if one citizen's self-interest is being enhanced, another citizen's self-interest is being diminished. The original thinking behind such a distortion of power was the belief that employees could only get justice, if they were to use such power against the evil employer.

And having helped to put socialists in charge of the state, they duly set about one evil employer after another. But hollow victory after hollow victory ensued, as one company after another went out of business. And it gradually dawned on a majority of the British electorate, that this enmity driven activity was not in their self-interest. It was not in their interest because anything obtained by force is not worth obtaining. Artificially secured wage rises loosened the structure that brought about subsequent collapse. The natural order cannot be obstructed, without the necessity of paying a heavy price for that obstruction. And now there are virtually no businesses that can withstand enmity driven activity from within; and remain in the market place.

But those where such activity still takes place are those which are isolated from the market place. The very citizens who fund their existence have now taken the place of the evil employer. But while the employer, being forced to capitulate, had the power to walk away, the citizen has no such power. While the state still allows distorted power, people stand shivering at bus stops in the swirling rain.

No such situation could persist if the population at large understood human nature. If each individual understood, that the self-interest that governed them, also governed everyone else; then they would not allow the banding together of some individuals to advance their own self-interest to the detriment of all others. And by no means insignificantly; motivationally structured incomes would be the norm rather than the exception. The best employers understand that, just as they are motivated by self-interest, so too are their employees.

Whatever the nature of the business, if remuneration is connected with performance there will be an inevitable improvement. People will work in their own self-interest, and the more their self-interest is served by their work, the more diligently they perform. Conversely, if remuneration is received regardless of performance, or regardless of absence, then the demotivational force produces a morale sapping mediocrity. It is also true that the attitude of any, and every human being, will change instantaneously depending on the assessment of their own self-interest. Therefore, it is only the manner in which one individual pursues their own self-interest, as opposed to another, that dictates the tenor of our lives.

Some observers have been too keen to point to difference in intelligence, culture or genetics. But these differences are nothing, compared with the differences created by the quality of parenting in the early years of life. This dictates the degree of anger and hostility or the degree of love and kindness that possess the individual throughout life. We are all driven by the same biological urges, and thanks to recent discoveries; we know we are far closer genetically to the fruit fly than most vanity transfixed philosophers would care to have accepted heretofore. And one might add vanity transfixed political ideologies. For there could only ever be justification for interference in nature if there was sufficient proof that we are a unique life form. Or as some believed that we were not part of nature, but nature was here to serve us. But now that we have incontrovertible evidence that we share in the region of eighty five percent of our genes with dogs, and ninety nine percent with chimpanzees, isn't it about time the interventionists learned some lessons?

But it will probably take some considerable time for these lessons to be learned. Because the greatest irony is that the misplaced appraisal of our own intelligence prevents us from using what little intelligence we have to appropriately position ourselves in nature. Had we been somehow able to do so; humanity would have had a more peaceful existence. And had we somehow been able to ensure that all children were raised by mature loving parents then war would have been impossible. If a man loved himself he could not set out to slaughter complete strangers in other countries who wanted precisely the same things in life as he did. But when psychologically defective persons become leaders of nations, war has often ensued. And war is a destructive process; a tearing down, just as any enmity driven activity is a tearing down.

A soldier standing motionless in a sodden trench in northern France, rifle held across his chest has just thought of his wife and child for the first time in five days. It is 1918. He is just one of twenty-five remaining from a battalion of six hundred men. He doesn't know if he is quite human any more. He stares blankly through the criss-crossed stakes and barbed wire toward the three-day-old body of his friend lying in the deep mud. He recalls the day they so enthusiastically joined up to fight the war to end all wars. The body is arrested in a prolonged convulsion. He had seen the same in other fallen comrades. Then – loud squealing; and a line of several rats run out of his body and disappear from view.

Each barrage of gunfire, each exploding shell, each feeding rat was this man's reality. A reality that became part of him. A reality that some treacherous philosophers pretended they sought to find. But what use Kant's nefarious noumena to this man? Kant could have engaged in an honest appraisal of human nature, but instead engaged in deception. He and his two successors; Hegel and Marx stole from the meagre contents of the granary of truth. And as such, were by no means unconnected with succeeding senseless wars.

Human life is one life, and all of that life is made up of unique individual human beings. And the belief that a group of human beings born in one country are superior to a group of human beings born in another country is a dangerous belief. And the belief that the contents of one religious book are right, and the contents of other religious books are wrong, is a dangerous belief.

A visitor from another galaxy would probably not be able to contain his laughter, on seeing what some people were prepared to do to others; because they did not hold the same indefensible beliefs as themselves. But while religious violence may continue, because the necessary objectivity to recognise flawed beliefs is not yet possible, no objectivity is required for enlightened governments to undermine violence in the most powerful manner. And they can do that by ensuring on the one hand, that they take no action to undermine the natural family unit. And to use every means at their disposal to disseminate the message of the imperative nature of the provision of unconditional love to children. For a child who receives no violence, can do no violence.

But no matter how forcefully an enlightened government were to disseminate such a message, there can be no possibility of the State intervening in particular cases of wanton neglect. For the wanton neglect of any child is the responsibility of the two persons who begot that child. And if they, are not concerned; no other citizen can be legitimately forced to have concern. But if individuals feel that they can usefully alleviate that neglect, then their voluntary intervention can be unbounded. However, no matter how passionately one feels about the welfare of children the expectation that the State can alleviate any case of neglect will be met with huge disappointment. For as soon as the state intervenes with other people's money, it gives rise to a hundred new cases, because of the knowledge that responsibility can be shifted to others.

The enlightened government must never capitulate to emotion, or to the intellectual pygmies, or to the clamouring brigade, whose war cry is that; "they should do something!" Those who make such a cry are announcing a belief in their own inferiority. They seem to believe that those who conduct the business of the state are superior human beings. They seem to believe that other people have the power to correct something that they themselves could not correct. Or perhaps they just believe that other people should spend other people's money trying to correct something that they in their wisdom believe to be correctable.

But people who make such a cry are not doers; they are passive complainers and blamers, who feel that a host of social ills could be eradicated, if only a group of unnamed individuals would just do something. However, the neglect of a child by two grown ups is not correctable by the expenditure of other people's taxes. The only wise course of action is to ensure a minimum of such cases by steadfast nonintervention. And should any criminal assault be an aspect of that neglect, then the law that exists to ensure the personal safety of all human beings ought to be used. The thinking that such persons would ever be amenable to pleasant words, from a host of civil servants from the social services departments, ought to have run its course of futility by now.

A mistake made far too often by too many people is the assessment of the unacceptability or otherwise of someone else's conditions in relation to their own standards. Or indeed the possible correctability of someone else's circumstances when the person to whom the circumstances are relevant sees no need of their correction. The attempt to push any individual citizen off their existing path is futile unenlightened intervention. Since that particular person is on their own path for reasons another would not fully understand. Unless an outsider is capable of getting inside another's head, and changing their psychological profile then the belief that they would be comfortable on another path is quite misguided. All citizens have to face their own challenges, and those who believe that state intervention should obviate the need of some citizens to face their own challenges, rather than doing a service, does a disservice.

Not only is this true of individual citizens, it is equally true of nation states. Some unenlightened citizens living in affluent nations look at people living in poverty stricken nations and think, "they should do something". And what they mean is that international governments ought to provide more aid; or ignore the repayment of existing loans. But if they would not walk around their local streets, cheque book in hand, wiping out the debts of their neighbours, one wonders why they see such logic in an international context. Do they perhaps feel that a government which has no regard for the welfare of its citizens on one day; is going to have regard the next day when international governments pay it to do so? Empathy is an aspect of one's psychological profile and cannot be affected by financial inducements. And if a country is using its resources to buy weapons to wage war on neighbouring countries then it would appear that the plight of its citizens; that so moves outsiders to comment, is not its highest priority. And a wise person therefore, would not wish to take any steps that would ensure the prolongation of war.

As individuals are involved in their own progression, so too are nation states. And no matter how slow and painful that may appear to an outsider they must be permitted to proceed unhindered. All nation states on earth are at their own stage of political evolution. It is perfectly clear that some are at a more advanced stage than others, and those that we may consider to be the more advanced have had a very painful past. And that pain was undoubtedly a necessary pain. Lessons have had to be learned by many nationalities. One of the more important ones being that; violence begets violence. Whether that being within national boundaries or without. And the most important lesson; that each person must be at liberty to pursue their own self-interest, without let or hindrance; and have an equal voice with every other person in the manner in which he is governed.

The advent of representative democracy has been the strongest force for improving the quality of people's lives. And even though many governments throughout the world have this evidence available to them, they choose not to use the information in their own countries. Without democracy a minority will always be prepared to do whatever it takes to maintain their position of privilege. The absence of democracy demonstrates a belief by those in government that they are superior to other human beings. They do not have sufficient empathy to understand that others have the same desires and needs regarding their own lives as they do themselves. And like all areas of offending which are derived from an empathy void, the failure to allow democratic government is an offence against a majority of citizens.

But it is only when dissatisfaction arises amongst sufficient numbers, who are then prepared to undertake the necessary effort to ensure that they themselves are empowered, will any change arise. For if democracy were somehow imposed from without, it would disappear as soon as it arrived. Since if people have not made the effort to bring something about, they will not value it once it arrives. So intervention by the state on behalf of the individual and intervention by some governments in other nation states are equally counter-productive.

Sometimes however the deleterious effects of the state's intervention on behalf of the individual are only indirectly observable. Some decades ago the socialists became very concerned indeed about a tiny number of citizens who found themselves in difficulties because of a failure to pay their rents. And an even smaller number found themselves in difficulties because of the ruthless and criminal behaviour of some landlords who raised rents to exorbitant levels in order to force tenants to leave. However, it is in the self-interest of any landlord to ensure that he has an amicable relationship with his tenants, who are his customers, and the criminal behaviour of the few was highly exceptional. And the behaviour of the few who had no empathy with their fellow human beings ought to have been good news for other landlords who had property available to rent.

But alas, because of the socialists' intervention, they ensured it became good news for themselves. Because of highly exceptional cases they enacted legislation that brought about the disappearance of most of the rentable accommodation in the entire country. In this legislation they were not just aligning themselves with the tiny few, but also with those who failed to pay agreed rents. And failure to pay agreed rents cannot be distinguished from stealing in any meaningful way. One of the reasons those laws found their way onto the statute book was because the socialists regarded any citizen with property to rent, as their natural enemy. And if he could be disadvantaged along with justifying the expansion in public housing, then they would have a twin pay-off.

But then the state, acting as the landlord on behalf of those who had funded the provision of public housing would surely have a duty to ensure rents were paid. A reasonable person might be excused for thinking so. But the state assumes no such duty. The message is that paying rent for the property in which one lives is a mere nicety of human behaviour and is not really necessary. So the tens of millions and hundred of millions of pounds of unpaid rent to local authorities throughout Britain will not be recovered. The socialists are perfectly happy that the shortfall will be made up by citizens who are not their natural supporters while the beneficiaries of the leniency are.

While some small number of citizens were on a path toward discovering that non payment of rent had adverse consequences, they were shifted from that path by the intervention. Not only were they prevented from learning, but encouraged in their new circumstances that their behaviour was justified. So instead of a small number failing to pay agreed rents, the intervention has meant a very large number failing to pay highly subsidised rents. The wrong has not only been magnified enormously; but the burden of rectifying the wrong has been transferred to those not responsible for it, by socialist intervention. Just like some countries never forgive the soldiers from other nations who fight on their soil and liberate them from an aggressor; similarly people do not forgive others from whom they can easily steal. No enlightened government could allow a situation to exist which chips away at responsibility and respect for others.

And while local authorities are lenient in some areas, and spend vast sums unnecessarily on others, they can close libraries to save a tiny sum, as part of some fictitious financial stringency. While libraries exist for the common good and are there for the educational and personal development of all citizens, they are the prime target for the diversion of funds, to the particular individual's assistance. This attracts votes; since it is in the interest of the assisted person to be fully aware of the political party which has been so generous with other people's money. And while on the one hand there is a strategy to create dependants, it is also wise to block off a possible avenue of personal improvement, which could mean an escape from dependency, and the possible support or another political party.

In all democracies however, enlightened government could rarely come about without it being the desire of an enlightened electorate. When someone who can be regarded as a great leader holds power in a nation it is as much by accident as design that they attain such a position. Since for a politician to rise to the top in a political party they must be considered favourably by other members of the party. And being considered favourably does not always result from having the necessary characteristics to be a great leader. Those who have courage, wisdom and understanding may not be highly popular with others. It will only be when politicians are representative of an enlightened electorate that enlightened government will follow. A people generally get the government they deserve. And when such a government comes into existence it could only govern to promote the common good.

One aspect of that common good where expenditure by the state may not necessarily directly benefit those citizens who have provided the taxation is in the area of education. But since the education of a nation's youth is in the long-term interest of the nation state, it can be justified as being in the interest of all. And while expenditure on education is being made on behalf of those children's parents, it is an expenditure to benefit the future adult population. And because those availing of the education service are not capable of being direct targets in the quest to elect politicians, no direct manipulation can arise. But no area can exist under enlightened government where the state can take money from some adult citizens to give to other adult citizens. While it is reasonable to fund education from general taxation the strongest possible measures would be undertaken in the multi-tier system to create a service provider and customer relationship.

The state would also have the duty to uphold law and order; the rationale for which has been so eloquently outlined by John Locke. It would also have the duty for the construction of all aspects of infrastructure which are the veins of a strong and vibrant economy. And while some may consider the defence of the nation not the great priority it once was; they would be falsely complacent.

There are many examples in history where great civilisations, while preoccupied with what could be regarded as higher pursuits, were not equipped to defend themselves from outside attack. Sooner or later they were overrun and subjugated by others. And invariably those who were subjugated were at a more advanced stage in their political evolution than their oppressors. So while Britons may consider that the time for international aggression has long gone, there are many in other nations who do not think likewise. There are many who will inevitably have to go through the learning process that violence begets violence, until they understand that peaceful coexistence is the better alternative.

Expenditure on the common good therefore encompasses four major areas; having excluded areas of vote buying. Then citizens would be free to take responsibility for their own lives as adults in an adult nation. However, without a written constitution; enlightened government could not remain for very long. Unless legitimate areas of government expenditure are outlined in explicit detail, there will always be politicians straining at the leash to use other people's money to buy votes. And such activity must be an impeachable offence in the new constitution. Only then will we have a state befitting the inheritance of Hobbes, Butler and Locke.

Bibliography

ARISTOTLE: The Nicomachean Ethics. J.A.K. Thomson Peguin Books 1955 (P.127)

BUTLER Jospeh: Sermons Upon Human Nature. Ed. Joe Angus (P.79)

DAWKINS Richard: The Selfish Gene. Oxford University Press 1989 (P.97, 139, 180, 198, 233)

HARRIS Thomas A.: The Book of Choice/I'm Ok – You're OK. Pan Books 1970 (P.223)

HUME David: A Treatise of Human Nature. Oxford University Press (Ed) David F. Norton and M.J. Norton. 2000 (Pp. 248, 255, 273, 293, 377)

LOCKE John: A Letter Concerning Toleration. Essay Concerning the True Original Extent and Purpose of Civil Government. William Benton/Encyclopaedia Britannica Inc.

MAYO Bernard: The Philosophy of Right and Wrong Routledge & Kegan Paul 1964 (P.61)

MIDGLEY Mary: Beast and Man. Methuen & Co. Ltd. 1980 (P.119-121)

MITCHINSON John: British Greats. Cassell & Co. 2000 (P.146)

PLOWDEN Lady: Report 1967: Central Advisory Council for Education.

SHAKESPEARE William: Hamlet, Act Two, Scene Two.

SHAW G.B.: Mrs. Warren's Profession

Supplementary Reading

BERNE Eric: Games People Play Penguin Books 1966

FREUD Sigmund: On Sexuality. The Penguin Freud Library Cen. Editors A. Richars, A. Dickson.

HOBBES Thomas: Leviathan Edited, with introduction by C.B. MacPherson.

HUME David: On Religion The Fontana Library 1963.

ISRAEL Paul: Edison, A Life of Invention John Wiley & Sons Inc. 1998

KANT Immanuel: Critique of Pure Reason   Translated by Norman Kemp-Smith. Palgrave.

LOCKE John: An Essay Concerning Human Understanding Penguin Classics 1997. Ed. Roger Woolhouse.

MACHIAVELLI Niccolo: The Prince. Cambridge University Press 1988 Ed. Q. Skinner and R. Price.

MURE G.R.G.: The Philosophy of Hegel Thoemes Press.

PIAGET Jean: The Psychology of Intelligence Translated by M. Piercy & D.E. Berlyne.

SCHLICK Moritz: Ethics and the Will Ed. Brian McGuinness. Kluwer Academic Publishers London 1994